POLITICS OF THE
NEW LEFT

The Insight Series
Studies in Contemporary Issues
from Glencoe Press

Series Editors: Fred Krinsky and Joseph Boskin

POLITICS OF THE NEW LEFT

Matthew Stolz

Assistant Professor
San Francisco State College

GLENCOE PRESS
A Division of The Macmillan Company
Beverly Hills, California
Collier-Macmillan Ltd., London

GLENCOE PRESS
A Division of The Macmillan Company
8701 Wilshire Boulevard
Beverly Hills, California 90211
Collier-Macmillan Canada, Ltd., Toronto, Canada

Library of Congress catalog number: 78-153660

First Printing, 1971

Contents

22065

INTRODUCTION

Politics without culture is pointless, culture without politics, defenseless.

This is not a history of the New Left, nor a study of its moral passion. It is, rather an investigation into the New Left's understanding of power and politics in America. The materials presented here attempt to demonstrate that, in the name of equality, the new American radicals have sought effective forms of action against the established powers. Contrary to recent criticisms, these people are not nihilists bent upon random destruction; the new radicals are this nation's present-day populists[1]:

"The New Left emerges as a class which perceives concentration of power, in whatever hands, as the main threat."[2]

Action against concentrations of power, action in the name of equality, action in defense of the powerless: these themes, both in terms of theory and practice have made this generation of radicals the most highly politicized in American history.

As a consequence of the New Left movement, the political life of the nation has broadened in scope — that is it has added to the political lexion the phrase "extraordinary politics." During the decade just past we have witnessed the growth of this kind of political action.

Prior to this renaissance of populist equality, normal, that is, electoral politics, had demanded a pragmatic accommodation to the existing power structure.

The sustaining values of the system were "agreement," moderation and "social peace."[3] Any attempt to seek a redistribution of power, to transcend normal politics was rejected. "It invites conflicts that can damage society."[4] The New Left, however, seeks to fashion new forms of action which would actually constitute a more meaningful equality: they seek a redistribution of power which would disrupt and perhaps dismantle the existing power structure.

The silence of the 1950's was shattered by the noise of marches, the rhetoric of sit-ins and teach-ins and America experienced both in the name of equality, and, as a response in defense of the established order.

As a result of these upheavals, it was learned that America possessed a history of violence directed against those who have struggled for an equal share of the nation's wealth.

The activities of the New Left have helped to clarify the nature of politics and power in America. But it has done more: it has urged upon the country as a whole an alternative image of democracy.

That the New Left has failed to give any kind of evidence of either concrete achievement of political sensibilities is a point willingly espoused by foes and reluctantly conceded by some of its friends — for example, the Old Left.

They fear that action without ideology, that is, action without a clear set of directives, will ultimately prove to be a useless passion: Liberals, on the other hand, fear the very existence of the extraordinary politics of the New Left.

> "Though not intended to destroy the democratic processes, civil disobedience tends plainly to impair their operation."[5]

For a moment, let us discuss the cultural aspects of the New Left: that is, in apolitical terms. Theodore Roszak, for example, praises the Left's personalism and quaisi tribal structure:

> "the young begin to speak of such impracticalities as 'community' and 'participatory democracy'; thus they revert to a style of human relations that characterizes village and tribe insisting that real politics"[6]

Real politics, however entail a "political end sought by no political means."[7] Roszak values the authenticity of New Left culture, not the problems it poses regarding power and democracy. Certainly it is true that together with the radical politics of the 1960's there emerged a counter-culture whose life style was the very antithesis of the American system.

This parallel development has permitted an interplay between politics and culture that is unique in American history. To a degree, it has even given to politics an aesthetic component.

> "The value emphasis of the new student radicals center on equality and freedom, but they do not stop there. They also include ... dignity; desire for beauty ... belief in cre-

ativity . . . ; wish for community and communal values . . . ;
preference for individuated, intensely felt, and self-
generated interpersonal style . . ."[8]

Nevertheless, the fact is that a culture lacking defense mechanisms
of one kind or another will be either absorbed or repressed. The defense of
a given culture as well as a move towards the assertion of equality can be
gained only through political means, that is, by adopting forms of action
which are political in nature.

The New Left provides a paradigm for viewing the contemporary
political scene. Alone, almost, among the forces at work in this society,
its members attempt to stir the energies of the populace.

"Resist!" "Let the people decide!" "All power to the
people."

These slogans hardly constitute a retreat into the peace and comfort
of middle America. Rather they indicate the Left's attempt to activate the
energies of popular power.

Its rhetoric affirms a Jeffersonian vision of the Republic. Involvement
means reclaiming the virtues of citizenship. When "power to the people"
is denied, the New Left would seek other modes of action through which
voices might be heard.

The New Left does indeed evoke an older populist tradition: it wel-
comes resistance.

"It prevents the degeneracy of government and nour-
ishes a general attention to public affairs."[9]

But unlike the populism of the late 19th century, this assertion of
equalities was directed not against an emerging capitalist plutocracy, but
against the elusive concept of corporate liberalism.[10]

For many whites, the Civil Rights movement formed the initial ideological thrust of their involvement in the Movement. For others, a rising
sense of frustration at not being able to alter the course of the war in
Vietnam stood as the foundation of their radicalization. As a consequence,
the ideology of the Left elaborates upon these experiences of impotence
and repression. In this sense, the members of the New Left are members
of the power elite: they structure America in terms of an oppressive
hierarchy and a vast power structure.

Americans often perceive the activities of the Left only in terms of noise
and disruptions. Nevertheless, there is more than mere noise: the ideology
out of which these actions emerge has its origin in the summation of

radical philosophy, sociology, and historiography as represented through the writings of the scholars Herbert Marcuse, C. Wright Mills, Gabriel Kolko and others. All share a pessimism regarding the history of power and democracy in America.

Their vision is this: together with a conservative crystallization of power in the hands of the few, this country has witnessed the exhaustion of all radical political opposition.

Historians of the New Left tend to reject the liberating image of reform politics. Consider, for example, the New Deal: "by accepting private property and federal assistance corporate capitalism was not prepared to effectively redistribute power or to extend equality from promise to reality."[11]

In the New Left political view, power serves the corporate structure, not the general population. From a New Left perspective, the American system has become a directorate of corporate power and governmental authority.

Liberals respond by saying that power in America is cushioned by welfare legislation. Asserting that economic security had replaced equality as a political issue, John Kenneth Galbraith asserted in 1958:

> "For the moment, we need only notice that as an economic and social goal, inequality has been declining in urgency and this has had its reflection in the conventional wisdom."[12]

Liberals tend to forget that in a capitalist society equality in a political sense threatens to or has actually become an anomaly. The New Left holds that the goals of modern America deny a populist vision. America, in their view, is divided into the managers and the managed.

> "The history of modern society may be readily understood as the story of the enlargement and the centralization of the means of power in economic, in political and in military institutions.[13]

Apologists for the existing power structure accuse the protesters of being Luddites,[14] lusting after a lost social Eden. Even critics of contemporary society appear awed at the "giant, routinized structures that defy fundamental alteration, and at the same time display an unchallengeable legitimacy."[15]

The New Left declares these institutions to be illegitimate. They defeat, by their very presence, democratic aspirations.

The problem, therefore, becomes one of action. How does one generate change in institutions that some fear "defy fundamental alteration."[16] The rhetoric of the New Left is clear: their vision demands a participatory democracy. But what kind of actions will restore this kind of democratic participation? Who, or what, will serve as the agent for change? At the beginning of the 1960's, C. Wright Mills deplored the "political idiocy"[17] of the American people. In his view, they seemed to lack any sense of public conscience. Other scholars supported his image of powerlessness by asserting that by "the mid-twenties socialism and populism had petered out...."[18] The radical farm and labor movements had long since been tamed and integrated into the structure of corporate liberalism.

Many Americans reject the possibility for radical change. The Left, it is argued, might possess a critique of American society but their ideology has been declared incomplete. They claim that no agent for radical change exists in America today. Nevertheless, the chief contribution of the New Left has been the creation of new styles of political action. All those elements which coalesce around the principle of equality, i.e., the black, the student militant, the war-resistor, the organized poor and the enraged professional who, metaphorically and literally, takes the long march through the institutions, become, potentially, the agents for radical change. The New Left seeks to politicize the active capacities of the people.

It is true that the Left has often been uncertain concerning tactics: must action, for example, only be non-violent? What if any, is the role of violence in a radical movement? Can there be a coalition with the blacks and with blue-collar workers or perhaps both? All on the Left, however, agree on the necessity for action. Action completes the ideology. Often, during the last decade, the New Left has flirted with "normal" electoral politics (the Scheer congressional campaign in Berkeley and the support given Eugene McCarthy are examples) but more fundamental has been its experiment with extraordinary forms of political action. Community organizing, non-violent direct action, war resistance — even street fighting — have more in common with the New Left than do normal politics. Electoral politics in New Left eyes reduces citizen participation to a minimum. The politics of the New Left are most clearly manifest through participation on the part of the individual. Against organized, that is "established" power, its opposition is manifest through its passion and sometimes its numbers. The activist becomes the hero of New Left politics.

The consideration of action dictates the structure of organization. Politics for the New Left becomes something akin to jazz in the sense that it becomes improvisational. The organization remains loose and decentralized; tactics, as well as organization, are improvised to suit new situations.

The New Left has, in effect, created this paradigm for viewing American politics: continuous sparring and occasional confrontations between elites who are capable of governing, and purposeful action by groups from the underlying population intent on disrupting that authority. Disruptions, the Left believes, can create situations in which those with the institutionalized power are compelled to listen to the demands of those without that power. The New Left asserts the need for a series of confrontations until a truly meaningful equality finds a satisfactory embodiment in the political life of the nation.

What judgment are we to make concerning the politics of the New Left? By 1970 many had claimed that the movement had failed. Nothing visible had been accomplished; besides, the Left had become factionalized and had turned against itself and the world. Irving Howe rejects the New Left as "the spoiled children of affluence."[19] They lack the patience, he claims, to build a movement and, out of frustration, turn to the "delirium of terrorist fantasy."[20] Before the response to the Cambodian invasion and the shootings at Kent State and Jackson, the following seemed a more generous judgment: as a movement, the New Left had failed to sustain itself, yet its actions had "opened many closed questions, forcing them into the arena of public controversy and making it 'safe' and politically profitable to adopt them as issues." However, the explosive response to Cambodia and to the on-campus death would dictate a more tentative conclusion.

The massive reaction on the campuses, in the streets, and in the nation at large suggests that the New Left has assisted in the creation of a new kind of political opposition in America. It is true that the initial opposition channeled its efforts into the normal political system (the emphasis being on petitions to the congress and on electoral politics), yet the complete range of action recapitulated the spectrum of the New Left experiment. During April and May of 1970 there were teach-ins, sit-ins, marches, community organizing, street-fighting: not just one form of action, but, rather, a symphony of actions. As of this writing, that symphony of actions—a refusal to obey a power that it deems illegitimate, along with a passion for resistance—is the legacy of the New Left.

As you read the articles in this anthology and hear the arguments, and seek a demonstration of their truth or falsity, remember the admonition of Thomas Hobbes that "when I shall set down my own reading orderly, and perspicuously, the pains left another will be only to consider, if he also find not the same in himself. For this kind of doctrine admitteth no other demonstration."[21] The truth of the anthology that follows is correct only insofar as it rests with one's own experiences of America, and perhaps in one's own passion for a more equal nation.

1. Populism: a 19th century political movement and party, strongly agrarian in orientation; supported economic reforms, opposed concentration of power in centralized institutions.
2. Rapoport, Anatol, "Have the Intellectuals a Class Interest?" *Recent Sociology*, ed., Hans Peter Dreitzel (London: The Macmillan Co., 1969), p. 228.
3. Dahl, Robert, *A Preface to Democratic Theory* (Chicago: The University of Chicago Press, 1964), p. 151.
4. Bell, Daniel, *The End of Ideology* (New York: Collier Books, 1962), p. 121.
5. Waskow, Arthur, *From Race-Riot to Sit-In* (Garden City: Doubleday and Co., 1966), p. 278.
6. To Establish Justice, To Insure Domestic Tranquility (New York: Award Books, 1969), p. 54.
7. Roszak, Theodore, *The Making of A Counter Culture* (Garden City: Doubleday and Co., 1969), p. 54.
8. Ibid., p. 267.
9. Gouldner, Alvin, The Coming Crisis of Western Sociology (New York: Basic Books, 1970), p. 399.
10. Corporate Liberalism: a term used to refer to the part of the corporate structure that holds a liberal set of structures.
11. Luddites: refers to members of a 16th century agrarian reform movement in England.
12. Koch, Adrienne, and Peden, William, *The Life and Selected Writings of Thomas Jefferson* (New York: Modern Library, 1944), p. 413.
13. Bernstein, Barton J., "The New Deal: The Conservative Achievements of Liberal Reform," *Towards a New Past*, Barton J. Bernstein, ed., (New York: Vintage Books, 1968), p. 202.
14. Galbraith, John Kenneth, *The Affluent Society* (Boston: Houghton Mifflin Co., 1968), p. 97.
15. Political Idiocy: a term used by the ancient Greeks to refer to one who was not a citizen, i.e., one who took no part in political activities.
16. Mills, C. Wright, "The Structure of Power in American Society," *Power Politics and People*, ed., Irving Horowitz (New York Ballantine Books, 1966), p. 25.
17. Wolin, Sheldon S. "Political Theory as a Vocation," *American Political Science Review*, #63, December 1969, p. 1076.
18. Lasch, Christopher, *The Agony of the American Left* (New York: Alfred A. Knopf, 1969), p. 1076.
19. Howe, Irving, "Political Terrorism: Hysteria on the Left," *The New York Times Magazine*, April 14, 1970, p. 27.
20. Schaar, John H. and Wolin, Sheldon S., "Where We Are Now," *The New York Review of Books*, May 7, 1970, p. 3.
21. Hobbes, Thomas, *The Leviathan* (New York: Collier Books, 1966), p. 20.

POLITICS OF THE
NEW LEFT

Chapter One

Ideology:
Democracy and Political Action

An analysis of a "power elite" and "corporate liberalism" within the context of American society generally ends by condemning concentrated and irresponsible power. A conservative America sustains poverty and racism at home and, in the world, stands a fearsome watch against revolutions. In this view, people are powerless to resist; making domestic and foreign policy has been taken out of their hands.

In the section that follows, the article by C. Wright Mills holds that the people are incapable of regaining their lost power. In the ancient Greek sense of the phrase, they have become "political idiots." In this context, Americans are a private people: they no longer aspire to the rights and responsibilities of citizenship.

In another vein, if Richard Flacks is correct, then the foundation for New Left action rests upon perceiving man as a citizen. The ideology of participatory democracy, Flacks says, in the name of equal citizenship, denies the legitimacy of elite rule and bureaucratic management. The New Left, he says, stands for a more equitable distribution of power in America.

Re-establishing a democracy, however, requires inventing effective forms of political action. The structure of corporate power, according to Flacks, must first be attacked, then dismantled. That, in the New Left view, calls for massive and direct confrontations. In concluding this section, Howard Zinn details the Left's commitment to action. He admits that the consequences of individual and group action cannot in any meaningful sense be calculated. According to Zinn, in the long run all our actions may be ineffective, or taken together they may culminate in a movement powerful enough to fracture the present American power structure, thereby liberating the democratic potential of its people.

The Structure of Power in American Society*

C. Wright Mills

I

Power has to do with whatever decisions men make about the arrangements under which they live, and about the events which make up the history of their times. Events that are beyond human decision do happen; social arrangements do change without benefit of explicit decision. But in so far as such decisions are made, the problem of who is involved in making them is the basic problem of power. In so far as they could be made but are not, the problem becomes who fails to make them?

We cannot today merely assume that in the last resort men must always be governed by their own consent. For among the means of power which now prevail is the power to manage and to manipulate the consent of men. That we do not know the limits of such power, and that we hope it does have limits, does not remove the fact that much power today is successfully employed without the sanction of the reason or the conscience of the obedient.

---

* British Journal of Sociology, reprinted with permission.

Surely nowadays we need not argue that, in the last resort, coercion is the "final" form of power. But then, we are by no means constantly at the last resort. Authority (power that is justified by the beliefs of the voluntarily obedient) and manipulation (power that is wielded unbeknown to the powerless)—must also be considered, along with coercion. In fact, the three types must be sorted out whenever we think about power.

In the modern world, we must bear in mind, power is often not so authoritative as it seemed to be in the medieval epoch: ideas which justify rulers no longer seem so necessary to their exercise of power. At least for many of the great decisions of our time—especially those of an international sort—mass "persuasion" has not been "necessary"; the fact is simply accomplished. Furthermore, such ideas as are available to the powerful are often neither taken up nor used by them. Such ideologies usually arise as a response to an effective debunking of power; in the United States such opposition has not been effective enough recently to create the felt need for new ideologies of rule.

There has, in fact, come about a situation in which many who have lost faith in prevailing loyalties have not acquired new ones, and so pay no attention to politics of any kind. They are not radical, not liberal, not conservative, not reactionary. They are inactionary. They are out of it. If we accept the Greek's definition of the idiot as an altogether private man, then we must conclude that many American citizens are now idiots. And I should not be surprised, although I do not know, if there were not some such idiots even in Germany. This—and I use the word with care—this spiritual condition seems to me the key to many modern troubles of political intellectuals, as well as the key to much political bewilderment in modern society. Intellectual "conviction" and moral "belief" are not necessary, in either the rulers or the ruled, for a ruling power to persist and and even to flourish. So far as the role of ideologies is concerned, their infrequent absences and the prevalence of mass indifference are surely two of the major political facts about the western societies today.

How large a role any explicit decisions do play in the making of history is itself an historical problem. For how large that role may be depends very much upon the means of power that are available at any given time in any given society. In some societies, the innumerable actions of innumerable men modify their milieux, and so gradually modify the structure itself. These modifications—the course of history—go on behind the backs of men. History is drift, although in total "men make it." Thus, innumerable entrepreneurs and innumerable consumers by ten-thousand decisions per minute may shape and re-shape the free-market economy. Perhaps this was the chief kind of limitation Marx had in mind when he wrote, in *The 18th Brumaire:* that "Men make their own history, but they do not make it just as they please; they do not make it under circumstances chosen by themselves. . . ."

But in other societies—certainly in the United States and in the Soviet Union today—a few men may be so placed within the structure that by their decisions they modify the milieux of many other men, and in fact nowadays the structural conditions under which most men live. Such elites of power also make history under circumstances not chosen altogether by themselves, yet compared with other men, and compared with other periods of world history, these circumstances do indeed seem less limiting.

I should contend that "men are free to make history," but that some men are indeed much freer than others. For such freedom requires access to the means of decision and of power by which history can now be made. It has not always been so made; but in the later phases of the modern epoch it is. It is with reference to this epoch that I am contending that if men do not make history, they tend increasingly to become the utensils of history-makers as well as the mere objects of history.

The history of modern society may readily be understood as the story of the enlargement and the centralization of the means of power—in economic, in political, and in military institutions. The rise of industrial society has involved these developments in the means of economic production. The rise of the nation-state has involved similar developments in the means of violence and in those of political administration.

In the western societies, such transformations have generally occurred gradually, and many cultural traditions have restrained and shaped them. In most of the Soviet societies, they are happening very rapidly indeed and without the great discourse of western civilization, without the Renaissance and without the Reformation, which so greatly strengthened and gave political focus to the idea of freedom. In those societies, the enlargement and the co-ordination of all the means of power has occurred more brutally, and from the beginning under tightly centralized authority. But in both types, the means of power have now become international in scope and similar in form. To be sure, each of them has its own ups and downs; neither is as yet absolute; how they are run differs quite sharply.

Yet so great is the reach of the means of violence, and so great the economy required to produce and support them, that we have in the immediate past witnessed the consolidation of these two world centers, either of which dwarfs the power of Ancient Rome. As we pay attention to the awesome means of power now available to quite small groups of men we come to realize that Caesar could do less with Rome than Napoleon with France; Napoleon less with France then Lenin with Russia. But what was Caesar's power at its height compared with the power of the changing inner circles of Soviet Russia and the temporary administrations of the United States? We come to realize— indeed they continually remind us—how a few men have access to the means by which in a few days continents can be turned into thermonuclear wastelands. That the facilities of power are so enormously enlarged and so decisively centralized surely means that the powers of quite small groups of men, which we may call elites, are now of literally inhuman consequence.

My concern here is not with the international scene but with the United States in the middle of the twentieth century. I must emphasize "in the middle of the twentieth century" because in our attempt to understand any society we come upon images which have been drawn from its past and which often confuse our attempt to confront its present reality. That is one minor reason why history is the shank of any social science: we must study it if only to rid ourselves of it. In the United States, there are indeed many such images and usually they have to do with the first half of the nineteenth century. At that time the economic facilities of the United States were very widely dispersed and subject to little or to no central authority.

The state watched in the night but was without decisive voice in the day.

One man meant one rifle and the militia were without centralized orders.

Any American, as old-fashioned as I, can only agree with

R. H. Tawney that "Whatever the future may contain, the past
has shown no more excellent social order than that in which the
mass of the people were the masters of the holdings which they
ploughed and the tools with which they worked, and could boast
... 'It is a quietness to a man's mind to live upon his own and to
know his heir certain.' "

But then we must immediately add: all that is of the past
and of little relevance to our understanding of the United States
today. Within this society three broad levels of power may now
be distinguished. I shall begin at the top and move downward.

II

The power to make decisions of national and international
consequences is now so clearly seated in political, military, and
economic institutions that other areas of society seem off to the
side and, on occasion, readily subordinated to these. The scattered
institutions of religion, education and family are increasingly
shaped by the big three, in which history-making decisions now
regularly occur. Behind this fact there is all the push and drive
of a fabulous technology; for these three institutional orders
have incorporated this technology and now guide it, even as it
shapes and paces their development.

As each has assumed its modern shape, its effects upon the
other two have become greater, and the traffic between the three
has increased. There is no longer, on the one hand, an economy,
and, on the other, a political order, containing a military establishment unimportant to politics and to money-making. There is
a political economy numerously linked with military order and
decision. This triangle of power is now a structural fact, and it
is the key to any understanding of the higher circles in America
today. For as each of these domains has coincided with the
others, as decisions in each have become broader, the leading
men of each—the high military, the corporation executives, the
political directorate—have tended to come together to form the
power elite of America.

The political order, once composed of several dozen states
with a weak federal center, has become an executive apparatus
which has taken up into itself many powers previously scattered,
legislative as well as administrative, and which now reaches into
all parts of the social structure. The long-time tendency of busi-

ness and government to become more closely connected has since World War II reached a new point of explicitness. Neither can now be seen clearly as a distinct world. The growth of executive government does not mean merely the "enlargement of government" as some kind of autonomous bureaucracy: under American conditions, it has meant the ascendency of the corporation man into political eminence. Already during the New Deal, such men had joined the political directorate; as of World War II they came to dominate it. Long involved with government, now they have moved into quite full direction of the economy of the war effort and of the post-war era.

The economy, once a great scatter of small productive units in somewhat automatic balance, has become internally dominated by a few hundred corporations, administratively and politically interrelated, which together hold the keys to economic decision. This economy is at once a permanent-war economy and a private-corporation economy. The most important relations of the corporation to the state now rest on the coincidence between military and corporate interests, as defined by the military and the corporate rich, and accepted by politicians and public. Within the elite as a whole, this coincidence of military domain and corporate realm strengthens both of them and further subordinates the merely political man. Not the party politician, but the corporation executive, is now more likely to sit with the military to answer the question: what is to be done?

The military order, once a slim establishment in a context of civilian distrust, has become the largest and most expensive feature of government; behind smiling public relations, it has all the grim and clumsy efficiency of a great and sprawling bureaucracy. The high military have gained decisive political and economic relevance. The seemingly permanent military threat places a premium upon them and virtually all political and economic actions are now judged in terms of military definitions of reality: the higher military have ascended to a firm position within the power elite of our time.

In part at least this is a result of an historical fact, pivotal for the years since 1939: the attention of the elite has shifted from domestic problems—centered in the 'thirties around slump —to international problems—centered in the 'forties and 'fifties around war. By long historical usage, the government of the

United States has been shaped by domestic clash and balance; it does not have suitable agencies and traditions for the democratic handling of international affairs. In considerable part, it is in this vacuum that the power elite has grown.

(i) To understand the unity of this power elite, we must pay attention to the psychology of its several members in their respective milieux. In so far as the power elite is composed of men of similar origin and education, of similar career and style of life, their unity may be said to rest upon the fact that they are of similar social type, and to lead to the fact of their easy intermingling. This kind of unity reaches its frothier apex in the sharing of that prestige which is to be had in the world of the celebrity. It achieves a more solid culmination in the fact of the interchangeability of positions between the three dominant institutional orders. It is revealed by considerable traffic of personnel within and between these three, as well as by the rise of specialized go-betweens as in the new style high-level lobbying.

(ii) Behind such psychological and social unity are the structure and the mechanics of those institutional hierarchies over which the political directorate, the corporate rich, and the high military now preside. How each of these hierarchies is shaped and what relations it has with the others determine in large part the relations of their rulers. Were these hierarchies scattered and disjointed, then their respective elites might tend to be scattered and disjointed; but if they have many interconnections and points of coinciding interest, then their elites tend to form a coherent kind of grouping. The unity of the elite is not a simple reflection of the unity of institutions, but men and institutions are always related; that is why we must understand the elite today in connection with such institutional trends as the development of a permanent-war establishment, alongside a privately incorporated economy, inside a virtual political vacuum. For the men at the top have been selected and formed by such institutional trends.

(iii) Their unity, however, does not rest solely upon psychological similarity and social intermingling, nor entirely upon the structural blending of commanding positions and common interests. At times it is the unity of a more explicit co-ordination.

To say that these higher circles are increasingly co-ordinated, that this is *one* basis of their unity, and that at times—as during open war—such co-ordination is quite wilful, is not to say that the co-ordination is total or continuous, or even that it is very surefooted. Much less is it to say that the power elite has emerged as the realization of a plot. Its rise cannot be adequately explained in any psychological terms.

Yet we must remember that institutional trends may be defined as opportunities by those who occupy the command posts. Once such opportunities are recognized, men may avail themselves of them. Certain types of men from each of these three areas, more far-sighted than others, have actively promoted the liaison even before it took its truly modern shape. Now more have come to see that their several interests can more easily be realized if they work together, in informal as well as in formal ways, and accordingly they have done so.

The idea of the power elite is of course an interpretation. It rests and it enables us to make sense of major institutional trends, the social similarities and psychological affinities of the men at the top. But the idea is also based upon what has been happening on the middle and lower levels of power, to which I now turn.

III

There are of course other interpretations of the American system of power. The most usual is that it is a moving balance of many competing interests. The image of balance, at least in America, is derived from the idea of the economic market: in the nineteenth century, the balance was thought to occur between a great scatter of individuals and enterprises; in the twentieth century, it is thought to occur between great interest blocs. In both views, the politician is the key man of power because he is the broker of many conflicting powers.

I believe that the balance and the compromise in American society—the "countervailing powers" and the "veto groups," of parties and associations, of strata and unions—must now be seen as having mainly to do with the middle levels of power. It is these middle levels that the political journalist and the scholar of politics are most likely to understand and to write about—if only because, being mainly middle class themselves, they are closer to them. Moreover these levels provide the noisy content of most "political" news and gossip; the images of these levels are more or less in accord with the folklore of how democracy works; and, if the master image of balance is accepted, many intellectuals, especially in their current patrioteering, are readily able to satisfy such political optimism as they wish to feel. Accordingly, liberal interpretations of what is happening in the United States are now virtually the only interpretations that are widely distributed.

But to believe that the power system reflects a balancing society is, I think, to confuse the present era with earlier times, and to confuse its top and bottom with its middle levels.

By the top levels, as distinguished from the middle, I intended to refer, first of all, to the scope of the decisions that are made. At the top today, these decisions have to do with all the issues of war and peace. They have also to do with slump and poverty which are now so very much problems of international scope. I intend also to refer to whether or not the groups that struggle politically have a chance to gain the positions from which such top decisions are made, and indeed whether their members do usually hope for such top national command. Most of the competing interests which make up the clang and clash of American politics are strictly concerned with their slice of the existing pie. Labor unions, for example, certainly have no policies of an international sort other than those which given unions adopt for the strict economic protection of their members. Neither do farm organizations. The actions of such middle-level powers may indeed have consequences for top-level policy; certainly at times they hamper these policies. But they are not truly concerned with them, which means of course that their influence tends to be quite irresponsible.

The facts of the middle levels may in part be understood in terms of the rise of the power elite. The expanded and centralized and interlocked hierarchies over which the power elite preside have encroached upon the old balance and relegated it to the middle level. But there are also independent developments of the middle levels. These, it seems to me, are better understood as an affair of entrenched and provincial demands than as a center of national decision. As such, the middle level often seems much more of a stalemate than a moving balance.

(i) The middle level of politics is not a forum in which there are debated the big decisions of national and international life. Such debate is not carried on by nationally responsible parties representing and clarifying alternative policies. There are no such parties in the United States. More and more, fundamental issues never come to any point or decision before the Congress, much less before the electorate in party campaigns. In the case of Formosa, in the spring of 1955 the Congress abdicated all debate concerning events and decisions which surely bordered on war. The same is largely true of the 1957 crisis in the Middle East. Such decisions now regularly by-pass the Congress, and are never clearly focused issues for public decision.

The American political campaign distracts attention from national and international issues, but that is not to say that there are no issues in these campaigns. In each district and state, issues are set up and watched by organized interests of sovereign local importance. The professional politician is of course a party politician, and the two parties are semifeudal organizations: they trade patronage and other favors for votes and for protection. The differences between them, so far as national issues are concerned, are very narrow and very mixed up. Often each seems to be fifty parties, one to each state; and accordingly, the politician as campaigner and as Congressman is not concerned with national party lines, if any are discernible. Often he is not subject to any effective national party discipline. He speaks for the interests of his own constituency, and he is concerned with national issues only in so far as they affect the interests effectively organized there, and hence his chances of re-election. That is why, when he does speak of national matters, the result is so often such an empty rhetoric. Seated in his sovereign locality, the politician is not at the national summit. He is on and of the middle levels of power.

(ii) Politics is not an arena in which free and independent organizations truly connect the lower and middle levels of society with the top levels of decision. Such organizations are not an effective and major part of American life today. As more people are drawn into the political arena, their associations become mass in scale, and the power of the individual becomes dependent upon them; to the extent that they are effective, they have become larger, and to that extent they have become less accessible to the influence of the individual. This is a central fact about associations in any mass society: it is of most consequence for political parties and for trade unions.

In the 'thirties, it often seemed that labor would become an insurgent power independent of corporation and state. Organized labor was then emerging for the first time on an American scale, and the only political sense of direction it needed was the slogan, "organize the un-organized." Now without the mandate of the slump, labor remains without political direction. Instead of economic and political struggles it has become deeply entangled in administrative routines with both corporation and state. One of its major functions, as a vested interest of the new society, is the regulation of such irregular tendencies as may occur among the rank and file.

There is nothing, it seems to me, in the make-up of the current labor leadership to allow us to expect that it can or that it will lead, rather than merely react. In so far as it fights at all it fights over a share of the goods of a single way of life and not over that way of life itself. The typical labor leader in the U.S.A. today is better understood as an adaptive creature of the main business drift than as an independent actor in a truly national context.

(iii) The idea that this society is a balance of powers requires us to assume that the units in balance are of more or less equal power and that they are truly independent of one another. These assumptions have rested, it seems clear, upon the historical importance of a large and independent middle class. In the latter nineteenth century and during the Progressive Era, such a class of farmers and small businessmen fought politically—and lost—their last struggle for a paramount role in national decision. Even then, their aspirations seemed bound to their own imagined past.

This old, independent middle class has of course declined. On the most generous count, it is now 40 per cent of the total middle class (at most 20 per cent of the total labor force). Moreover, it has become politically as well as economically dependent upon the state, most notably in the case of the subsidized farmer.

The *new* middle class of white-collar employees is certainly not the political pivot of any balancing society. It is in no way politically unified. Its unions, such as they are, often serve merely to incorporate it as hanger-on of the labor interest. For a considerable period, the old middle class *was* an independent base of power; the new middle class cannot be. Political freedom and economic security *were* anchored in small and independent properties; they are not anchored in the worlds of the white-collar job. Scattered property holders were economically united by more or less free markets; the jobs of the new middle class are integrated by corporate authority. Economically, the white-collar classes are in the same condition as wage workers; politically, they are in a worse condition, for they are not organized. They are no vanguard of historic change; they are at best a rear-guard of the welfare state.

The agrarian revolt of the 'nineties, the small-business revolt that has been more or less continuous since the 'eighties, the labor revolt of the 'thirties—each of these has failed as an independent movement which could countervail against the powers that be; they have failed as politically autonomous third parties. But they have succeeded, in varying degree, as interests vested in the expanded corporation and state; they have succeeded as parochial interests seated in particular districts, in local divisions of the two parties, and in the Congress. What they would become, in short, are well-established features of the *middle* levels of balancing power, on which we may now observe all those strata and interests which in the course of American history have been defeated in their bids for top power or which have never made such bids.

Fifty years ago many observers thought of the American state as a mask behind which an invisible government operated. But nowadays, much of what was called the old lobby, visible or invisible, is part of the quite visible government. The "governmentalization of the lobby" has proceeded in both the legislative and the executive domain, as well as between them. The executive bureaucracy becomes not only the center of decision but also the arena within which major conflicts of power are resolved or denied resolution. "Administration" replaces electoral politics; the maneuvering of cliques (which include leading Senators as well as civil servants) replaces the open clash of parties.

The shift of corporation men into the political directorate

has accelerated the decline of the politicians in the Congress to the middle levels of power; the formation of the power elite rests in part upon the relegation. It rests also upon the semi-organized stalemate of the interests of sovereign localities, into which the legislative function has so largely fallen; upon the virtually complete absence of a civil service that is a politically neutral but politically relevant, depository of brain-power and executive skill; and it rests upon the increased official secrecy behind which great decision are made without benefit of public or even of Congressional debate.

IV

There is one last belief upon which liberal observers everywhere base their interpretations and rest their hopes. That is the idea of the public and the associated idea of public opinion. Conservative thinkers, since the French Revolution, have of course Viewed With Alarm the rise of the public, which they have usually called the masses, or something to that effect. "The populace is sovereign," wrote Gustave LeBon, "and the tide of barbarism mounts." But surely those who have supposed the masses to be well on their way to triumph are mistaken. In our time, the influence of publics or of masses within political life is in fact decreasing, and such influence as on occasion they do have tends, to an unknown but increasing degree, to be guided by the means of mass communication.

In a society of publics, discussion is the ascendant means of communication, and the mass media, if they exist, simply enlarge and animate this discussion, linking one face-to-face public with the discussions of another. In a mass society, the dominant type of communication is the formal media, and publics become mere markets for these media: the "public" of a radio program consists of all those exposed to it. When we try to look upon the United States today as a society of publics, we realize that it has moved a considerable distance along the road to the mass society.

In the official circles, the very term, "the public," has come to have a phantom meaning, which dramatically reveals its eclipse. The deciding elite can identify some of those who clamor publicly as "Labor," others as "Business," still others as "Farmer." But these are not the public. "The public" consists of the unidentified and the nonpartisan in a world of defined and partisan interests. In this faint echo of the classic notion, the public is composed of these remnants of the old and new middle classes whose interests are not explicitly defined, organized, or clamorous. In a curious adaptation, "the public" often becomes, in administrative fact, "the disengaged expert," who, although never so well informed, has never taken a clear-cut and public stand on controversial issues. He is the "public" member of the board, the commission, the committee. What "the public" stands for, accordingly, is often a vagueness of policy (called "open-mindedness"), a lack of involvement in public affairs (known as "reasonableness"), and a professional disinterest (known as "tolerance").

All this is indeed far removed from the eighteenth-century idea of the public of public opinion. The idea parallels the economic idea of the magical market. Here is the market composed for freely competing entrepreneurs; there is the public composed of circles of people in discussion. As price is the result of anonymous, equally weighted, bargaining individuals, so public opinion is the result of each man's having thought things out for himself and then contributing his voice to the great chorus. To be sure, some may have more influence on the state of opinion than others, but no one group monopolizes the discussion, or by itself determines the opinions that prevail.

In this classic image, the people are presented with problems. They discuss them. They formulate viewpoints. These viewpoints are organized, and they compete. One viewpoint "wins out." Then the people act on this view, or their representatives are instructed to act it out, and this they promptly do.

Such are the images of democracy which are still used as working justifications of power in America. We must now recognize this description as more of a fairy tale than a useful approximation. The issues that now shape man's fate are neither raised nor decided by any public at large. The idea of a society that is at bottom composed of publics is not a matter of fact; it is the proclamation of an ideal, and as well the assertion of a legitimation masquerading as fact.

I cannot here describe the several great forces within American society as well as elsewhere which have been at work in the debilitation of the public. I want only to remind you that publics, like free associations, can be deliberately and suddenly smashed, or they can more slowly wither away. But whether smashed in a week or withered in a generation, the demise of the public must be seen in connection with the rise of centralized organizations, with all their new means of power, including those of the mass media of distraction. These, we now know, often seem to expropriate the rationality and the will of the terrorized or—as the case may be—the voluntarily indifferent society of masses. In the more democratic process of indifference the remnants of such publics as remain may only occasionally be intimidated by fanatics in search of "disloyalty." But regardless of that, they lose their will for decision because they do not possess the instruments for decision; they lose their sense of political belonging because they do not belong; they lose their political will because they see no way to realize it.

The political structure of a modern democratic state requires that such a public as is projected by democratic theorists not only exist but that it be the very forum within which a politics of real issues is enacted.

It requires a civil service that is firmly linked with the world of knowledge and sensibility, and which is composed of skilled men who, in their careers and in their aspirations, are truly independent of any private, which is to say, corporation, interests.

It requires nationally responsible parties which debate openly and clearly the issues which the nation, and indeed the world, now so rigidly confronts.

It requires an intelligentsia, inside as well as outside the universities, who carry on the big discourse of the western world, and whose work is relevant to and influential among parties and movements and publics.

And it certainly requires, as a fact of power, that there be free associations standing between families and smaller communities and publics, on the one hand, and the state, the military, the corporation, on the other. For unless these do exist, there are no vehicles for reasoned opinion, no instruments for the rational exertion of public will.

Such democratic formations are not now ascendant in the power structure of the United States, and accordingly the men of decision are not men selected and formed by careers within such associations and by their performance before such publics. The top of modern American society is increasingly unified, and often seems wilfully coordinated: at the top there has emerged an elite whose power probably exceeds that of any small group of men in world history. The middle levels are often a drifting set of stalemated forces: the middle does not link the bottom with the top. The bottom of this society is politically fragmented, and even as a passive fact, increasingly powerless: at the bottom there is emerging a mass society.

These developments, I believe, can be correctly understood neither in terms of the liberal nor the Marxian interpretation of politics and history. Both these ways of thought arose as guidelines to reflection about a type of society which does not now exist in the United States. We confront there a new kind of social structure, which embodies elements and tendencies of all modern society, but in which they have assumed a more naked and flamboyant prominence.

That does not mean that we must give up the ideals of these classic political expectations. I believe that both have been concerned with the problem of rationality and freedom: liberalism, with freedom and rationality as supreme facts about the individual; Marxism, as supreme facts about man's role in the political making of history. What I have said here, I suppose, may be taken as an attempt to make evident why the ideas of freedom and of rationality now so often seem so ambiguous in the new society of the United States of America.

Trapped in a System

Carl Oglesby

[The speech delivered by Carl Oglesby, then president of SDS, at the October 27, 1965, antiwar march in Washington,

has become a classic in the New Left because of its open indictment of corporate liberalism. In its various reprintings, the
speech has been entitled either "Trapped in a System" or "Let
Us Shape the Future."]

Seven months ago at the April March on Washington, Paul
Potter, then President of Students for a Democratic Society,
stood in approximately this spot and said that we must name the
system that creates and sustains the war in Vietnam—name it,
describe it, analyze it, understand it, and change it.

Today I will try to name it—to suggest an analysis which, to
be quite frank, may disturb some of you—and to suggest what
changing it may require of us.

We are here again to protest again a growing war. Since it is
a very bad war, we acquire the habit of thinking that it must be
caused by very bad men. But we only conceal reality, I think,
by denouncing on such grounds the menacing coalition of industrial and military power, or the brutality of the blitzkrieg we are
waging against Vietnam, or the ominous signs around us that
heresy may soon no longer be permitted. We must simply observe,
and quite plainly say that this coalition, this blitzkrieg, and this
demand for acquiescence are creatures, all of them, of a Government that since 1932 has considered itself to be fundamentally
liberal.

The original commitment in Vietnam was made by President
Truman, a mainstream liberal. It was seconded by President
Eisenhower, a moderate liberal. It was intensified by the late
President Kennedy, a flaming liberal. Think of the men who now
engineer that war—those who study the maps, give the com-
mands, push the buttons, and tally the dead: Bundy, McNamara,
Rusk, Lodge, Goldberg, the President himself.

They are not moral monsters.

They are all honorable men.

They are all liberals.

But so, I'm sure, are many of us who are here today in
protest. To understand the war, then, it seems necessary to
take a closer look at this American liberalism. Maybe we are
in for some surprises. Maybe we have here two quite different
liberalisms: one authentically humanist; the other not so human
at all.

Not long ago, I considered myself a liberal. And if someone had asked me what I mean by that, I'd perhaps have quoted Thomas Jefferson or Thomas Paine, who first made plain our nation's unprovisional commitment to human rights. But what do you think would happen if these two heroes could sit down now for a chat with President Johnson and McGeorge Bundy?

They would surely talk of the Vietnam war. Our dead revolutionaries would soon wonder why their country was fighting against what appeared to be a revolution. The living liberals would hotly deny that it is one: there are troops coming in from outside, the rebels get arms from other countries, most of the people are not on their side, and they practice terror against their own. Therefore, *not* a revolution.

What would our dead revolutionaries answer? They might say: "What fools and bandits, sirs, you make then of us. Outside help? Do you remember Lafayette? Or the 3,000 British freighters the French navy sunk for our side? Or the arms and men we got from France and Spain? And what's this about terror? Did you never hear what we did to our own loyalists? Or about the thousands of rich American Tories who fled for their lives to Canada? And as for popular support, do you not know that we had less than one-third of our people with us? That, in fact, the colony of New York recruited more troops for the British than for the revolution? Should we give it all back?"

Revolutions do not take place in velvet boxes. They never have. It is only the poets who make them lovely. What the National Liberation Front is fighting in Vietnam is a complex and vicious war. This war is also a revolution, as honest a revolution as you can find anywhere in history. And this is a fact which all our intricate official denials will never change.

But it doesn't make any difference to our leaders anyway. Their aim in Vietnam is really much simpler than this implies. It is to safeguard what they take to be American interests around the world against revolution or revolutionary change, which they always called Communism—as if it were that. In the case of Vietnam, this interest is, first, the principle that revolution shall not be tolerated anywhere, and second, that South Vietnam shall never sell its rice to China—or even to North Vietnam.

There is simply no such thing now, for us, as a just revolution—never mind that for two-thirds of the world's people the 20th Century might as well be the Stone Age; never mind the melting poverty and hopelessness that are the basic facts of life for most modern men; and never mind that for these millions there is now an increasingly perceptible relationship between their sorrow and our contentment.

Can we understand why the Negroes of Watts rebelled? Then why do we need a devil theory to explain the rebellion of the South Vietnamese? Can we understand the oppression in Mississippi, or the anguish that our Northern ghettos make epidemic? Then why can't we see that our proper human struggles is not with Communism or revolutionaries, but with the social desperation that drives good men to violence, both here and abroad?

To be sure, we have been most generous with our aid, and in Western Europe, a mature industrial society, that aid worked. But there are always political and financial strings. And we have never shown ourselves capable of allowing others to make those traumatic institutional changes that are often the prerequisites of progress in colonial societies. For all our official feeling for the millions who are enslaved to what we so self-righteously call the yoke of Communist tyranny, we make no real effort at all to crack through the much more vicious right-wing tyrannies that our businessmen traffic with and our nation profits from every day. And for all our cries about the internnational Red conspiracy to take over the world, we take only pride in the fact of our 6,000 military bases on foreign soil.

We gave Rhodesia a grave look just now—but we keep on buying her chromium, which is cheap because black slave labor mines it.

We deplore the racism of Verwoerd's fascist South Africa— but our banks make big loans to that country and our private technology makes it a nuclear power.

We are saddened and puzzled by random back page stories of revolt in this or that Latin American state—but are convinced by a few pretty photos in the Sunday supplement that things are getting better, that the world is coming our way, that change from disorder can be orderly, that our benevolence will pacify the distressed, that our might will intimidate the angry.

Optimists, may I suggest that these are quite unlikely fantasies. They are fantasies because we have lost that mysterious social desire for human equity that from time to time has given us genuine moral drive. We have become a nation of young, bright-eyed, hard-hearted, slim-waisted, bullet-headed make-out artists. A nation—may I say it?—of beard-less liberals.

You say I am being hard? Only think.

This country, with its thirty-some years of liberalism, can send 200,000 young men to Vietnam to kill and die in the most dubious of wars, but it cannot get 100 voter registrars to go into Mississippi.

What do you make of it?

The financial burden of the war obliges us to cut millions from an already pathetic War on Poverty budget. But in almost the same breath, Congress appropriates $140 million for the Lockheed and Boeing companies to compete with each other on the supersonic transport project—that Disneyland creation that will cost us all about $2 billion before it's done.

What do you make of it?

Many of us have been earnestly resisting for some years now the idea of putting atomic weapons into West German hands, an action that would perpetuate the division of Europe and thus the Cold War. Now just this week we find out that, with the meagerest of security systems, West Germany has had nuclear weapons in her hands for the past six years.

What do you make of it?

Some will make of it that I overdraw the matter. Many will ask: What about the other side? To be sure, there is the bitter ugliness of Czechoslovakia, Poland, those infamous Russian tanks in the streets of Budapest. But my anger only rises to hear some say that sorrow cancels sorrow, or that *this* one's shame deposits in *that one's* account the right to shamefulness.

And others will make of it that I sound mighty anti-American. To these, I say: Don't blame *me* for *that!* Blame those who mouthed my liberal values and broke my American heart.

Just who might they be, by the way? Let's take a brief factual inventory of the latter-day Cold War.

In 1953 our Central Intelligence Agency managed to overthrow Mossadegh in Iran, the complaint being his neutralism in the Cold War and his plans to nationalize the country's oil resources to improve his peoples lives. Most evil aims, most evil man. In his place we put in General Zahedi, a World War II Nazi collaborator. New arrangements on Iran's oil gave 25-year leases on 40% of it to three U.S. firms, one of which was Gulf Oil. The CIA's leader for this coup was Kermit Roosevelt. In 1960 Kermit Roosevelt became a vice president of Gulf Oil.

In 1954, the democratically elected Arbenz of Guatemala wanted to nationalize a portion of United Fruit Company's plantations in his country, land he needed badly for a modest program of agrarian reform. His government was overthrown in a CIA-supported right-wing coup. The following year, Gen. Walter Bedell Smith, director of the CIA when the Guatemala venture was being planned, joined the board of directors of the United Fruit Company.

Comes 1960 and Castro cries we are about to invade Cuba. The Administration sneers, "poppycock," and we Americans believe it. Comes 1961 and the invasion. Comes with it the awful realization that the United States Government had lied.

Comes 1962 and the missile crisis, and our Administration stands prepared to fight global atomic war on the curious principle that another state does not have the right to its own foreign policy.

Comes 1963 and British Guiana, where Cheddi Jagan wants independence from England and a labor law modelled on the Wagner Act. And Jay Lovestone, the AFL-CIO foreign policy chief, acting, as always, quite independently of labor's rank and file, arranges with our Government to finance an eleven-week dock strike that brings Jagan down, ensuring that the state will remain *British* Guiana, and that any workingman who wants a wage better than 50c a day is a dupe of Communism.

Comes 1964. Two weeks after Under Secretary Thomas Mann announces that we have abandoned the *Alianza's* principle of no aid to tyrants, Brazil's Goulart is overthrown by the vicious right-winger, Ademar Barros, supported by a show of American gunboats at Rio de Janeiro. Within 24 hours, the new head of state, Mazzilli, receives a congratulatory wire from our President.

Comes 1965. The Dominican Republic. Rebellion in the streets. We scurry to the spot with 20,000 neutral Marines and our neutral peacemakers—like Ellsworth Bunker, Jr., Ambassador to the Organization of American States. Most of us know that our neutral Marines fought openly on the side of the junta, a fact that the Administration still denies. But how many also know that what was at stake was our new Caribbean Sugar Bowl? That this same neutral peacemaking Bunker is a board member and stock owner of the National Sugar Refining Company, a firm his father founded in the good old days, and one which has a major interest in maintaining the status quo in the Dominican Republic? Or that the President's close personal friend and advisor, our new Supreme Court Justice Abe Fortas, has sat for the past 19 years on the board of the Sucrest Company, which imports black-strap molasses from the Dominican Republic? Or that the rhetorician of corporate liberalism and the late President Kennedy's close friend Adolf Berle, was chairman of that same board? Or that our roving ambassador Averell Harriman's brother Roland is on the board of National Sugar? Or that our former ambassador to the Dominican Republic, Joseph Farland is a board member of the South Puerto Rico Sugar Co., which owns 275,000 acres of rich land in the Dominican Republic and is the largest employer on the island— at about one dollar a day?

Neutralists! God save the hungry people of the world from such neutralists!

We do not say these men are evil. We say rather, that good men can be divided from their compassion by the institutional system that inherits us all. Generation in and out, we are put to use. People become instruments. Generals do not hear the screams of the bombed; sugar executives do not see the misery of the cane cutters—for to do so is to be that much *less* the general, that much *less* the executive.

The foregoing facts of recent history describe one main aspect of the estate of Western liberalism. Where is our American humanism here? What went wrong?

Let's stare our situation coldly in the face. All of us are born to the colossus of history, our American corporate system—in many ways, an awesome organism. There is one fact that describes it: With about 5% of the world's people, we consume about half the world's goods. We take a richness that is in good part not our own, and we put it in our pockets, our garages, our split-levels, our bellies, and our futures.

On the *face* of it, it is a crime that so few should have so much at the expense of so many. Where is the moral imagination so abused as to call this just? Perhaps many of us feel a bit uneasy in our sleep. We are not after all, a cruel people. And perhaps we don't really need this super-dominance that deforms others. But what can we do? The investments are made. The financial ties are established. The plants abroad are built. Our system *exists*. One is swept up into it. How intolerable—to be born moral, but addicted to a stolen and maybe surplus luxury. Our goodness threatens to become counterfeit before our eyes—unless we change. But change threatens us with uncertainty—at least.

Our problem, then, is to justify this system and give its theft another name—to make kind and moral what is neither, to perform some alchemy with language that will make this injustice seem to be a most magnanimous gift.

A hard problem. But the Western democracies, in the heyday of their colonial expansionism, produced a hero worthy of the task.

Its name was free enterprise, and its partner was an *illiberal liberalism* that said to the poor and the dispossessed: What we acquire of your resources we repay in civilization. The white man's burden. But this was too poetic. So a much more hard-headed theory was produced. This theory said that colonial status is in fact a *boon* to the colonized. We give them technology and bring them into modern times.

But this deceived no one but ourselves. We were delighted with this new theory. The poor saw in it merely an admission that their claims were irrefutable. They stood up to us, without gratitude. We were shocked—but also confused, for the poor seemed again to be right. How long is it going to be the case, we wondered, that the poor will be right and the rich will be wrong?

Liberalism faced a crisis. In the face of the collapse of the European empires, how could it continue to hold together our twin need for richness and righteousness? How can we continue to sack the ports of Asia and still dream of Jesus?

The challenge was met with a most ingenious solution: the ideology of anti-Communism. This was the bind: we cannot call revolution bad, because we started that way ourselves, and because it is all too easy to see why the depossessed should rebel. So we will call revolution *Communism*. And we will reserve for ourselves the right to say what Communism means. We take note of revolution's enormities, wrenching them where necessary from their historical context and often exaggerating them, and say: Behold, Communism is a bloodbath. We take note of those reactionaries who stole the revolution, and say: Behold, Communism is a betrayal of the people. We take note of the revolution's need to consolidate itself, and say: Behold, Communism is a tyranny.

It has been all these things, and it will be these things again, and we will never be at a loss for those tales of atrocity that comfort us so in our self-righteousness. Nuns will be raped and bureaucrats will be disembowelled. Indeed, revolution is a fury. For it is a letting loose of outrages pent up sometimes over centuries. But the more brutal and longer-lasting the suppression of this energy, all the more ferocious will be its explosive release.

Far from helping Americans deal with this truth, the anti-Communist ideology merely tries to disguise it so that things may stay the way they are Thus, it depicts our presence in other lands not as a coercion, but a protection. It allows us even to say that the napalm in Vietnam is only another aspect of our humanitarian love—like those exorcisms in the Middle Ages that so often killed the patient. So we say to the Vietnamese peasant, the Cuban intelluctual, the Peruvian worker: "You are better dead than Red. If it hurts or if you don't understand why—sorry about that."

This is the action of *corporate liberalism*. It performs for the corporate state a function quite like what the Church once performed for the feudal state. It seeks to justify its burdens and protect it from change. As the Church exaggerated this office in the Inquisition, so with liberalism in the McCarthy time—which, if it was a reactionary phenomenon, was still made possible by our anti-Communist corporate liberalism.

Let me then speak directly to humanist liberals. If my facts are wrong, I will soon be corrected. But if they are right, then you may face a crisis of conscience. Corporatism or humanism: which? For it has come to that. Will you let your dreams be used? Will you be grudging apologist for the corporate state? Or will you help try to change it—not in the name of this or that blueprint or "ism," but in the name of simple human decency and democracy and the vision that wise and brave men saw in the time of our own revolution?

And if your commitment to human value is unconditional, then disabuse yourselves of the notion that statements will bring change, if only the right statements can be written, or that interviews with the mighty will bring change if only the mighty can be reached, or that marches will bring change if only we can make them massive enough, or that policy proposals will bring change if only we can make them responsible enough.

We are dealing now with a colossus that does not want to be changed. It will not change itself. It will not cooperate with those who want to change it. Those allies of ours in the Government—are they really our allies? If they *are,* then they don't need advice, they need *constituencies;* they don't need study groups, they need a *movement.* And if they are *not,* then all the more reason for building that movement with a most relentless conviction.

There are people in this country today who are trying to build that movement, who aim at nothing less than a humanist reformation. And the humanist liberals must understand that it is this movement with which their own best hopes are most in tune. We radicals know that the same history that you liberals know, and we can understand your occasional cynicism, exasperation, and even distrust. But we ask you to put these aside and help us risk a leap. Help us find enough time for the enormous work that needs doing here. Help us build. Help us shake the future in the name of plain human hope.

On the Uses of Participatory Democracy*

by Richard Flacks

1. The most frequently heard phrase used for defining participatory democracy is that "men must share in the decision which affect their lives." In other words, participatory democrats take very seriously *a vision of man as citizen;* and by taking seriously such a vision, they *seek to extend the conception of citizenship* beyond the conventional *political sphere to all institutions.* Other ways of stating the core values are to assert the following: each man has responsibility for the action of the institutions in which he is imbedded; all authority ought to be responsible to those "under" it; each man can and should be a center of power and initiative in society.

2. The first priority for the achievement of a democracy of participation is to win full political rights and representation for all sectors of the population. Democracy, in fact, is an issue for this generation of radicals largely because their political experience has been shaped by the Negroes' elemental struggle for a political voice in the U.S. This struggle has not been simply for the right to vote—though even this right has not yet been guaranteed—but, more broadly, it has been an effort to win a share of political power by poor Negroes. It has been the experience of Negroes in the North, where voting rights have been formally guaranteed, that Negroes as a group have remained systematically under-represented in the political process and that, where Negro representation exists, it operates in behalf of Negro middle-class interests and is highly dependent on the beneficence of white-dominated political machines. The results of this situation are plain to see in every Northern city. Thus the main thrust of radicals in the civil rights movement has to do less with breaking the barriers of legal segregation and formal exclusion than with

---

* Dissent, December, 1969. Reprinted with permission.

attempting to build viable grass-roots organizations of poor
Negroes, which would actually represent the needs of the
poor and remain independent of white and middle-class domination. The ideology of "participatory democracy" has been
useful in this effort, since it provides a rationale for avoiding
premature "coalition" of grass-roots groups with more powerful white or middle-class organizaations, for effectively criti-
cizing "charismatic" styles of leadership which prevent
rank-and-file people from learning political skills, for critizing
tendencies toward bureaucratism, demagoguery, and elitism
which are predictable in mass movements. Moreover, "participatory democracy," unlike black nationalist ideology, which
also helps to mobilize grass-roots Negroes, offers a possible
bridge between Negroes and other groups of poor or voiceless
people. Thus we find much of the same rhetoric and organizing
technique being used by SNCC workers in Southern Negro
communities, SDS organizers among poor whites in Chicago
and Cleveland, and farm labor organizers among the multi-
national grape workers in California.

Just how is participatory democracy being applied to the
organization of economically disadvantaged groups? It has
influenced the analysis of the problem of poverty in an affluent
society, by stressing lack of organization as a root cause of
deprivation. This analysis leads to an emphasis on grass-roots
political voicelessness and organization and mobilization of the
poor as the main way of ending poverty. Since the people
involved lack political skill, organization requires a full-time
staff, initially composed of students and ex-students, but soon
involving "indigenous" leadership. This staff has the problem
of allaying the fear, suspicion, and sense of inadequacy of the
community—hence there has been a strong emphasis on building a sense of community between staff and rank-and-file, and
of finding techniques which will facilitate self-expression, enable new leadership to emerge, enable people to gain dignity
by participation, and the organization to become self-sustaining.
Such techniques include: rotation of leadership, eschewing
by staff of opportunities to "speak for" the organization, the
use of "consensus" to foster expression by the less-articulate.

More important than such procedural techniques has been
the attempt to generate institutions which help to bind people

to the organization, to see immediate benefits from participation. Thus, in Mississippi, alongside the political organization
(the Freedom Democratic party), a variety of related "projects" have grown up—community centers, freedom schools,
a Poor People's Corporation to help finance small business
enterprise, cooperatives, and the like. In Newark, the Newark
Community Union has established its own radio station. In
California, the Farm Worker Association established a credit
union. In Cleveland, the SDS Community Project established
a traveling street theater. Although these new institutions are
sometimes viewed as alternatives to participation in "organized society" (*vide* Staughton Lynd in DISSENT—Summer,
1965), in practice, they are a very important way of sustaining a developing organization. They enable people to participate
in an organization in a continuing fashion, help develop organizational resources, train people for leadership, and give people
a sense of the possibilities for social change. But they are in
no sense a *substitute* for political activity, direct action, and
the development of a program. These, and not the devolop-
ment of "parallel institutions," constitute the main functions
of the local political parties, community unions. etc., which
are developing in many urban slum and rural areas.

The emphasis on participatory democracy has helped these
developing grass-roots organizations formulate and articulate
issues and programs. Although the constituencies of these
organizations include the most impoverished sectors of society,
it is remarkable that—particularly in the Northern cities—
the main activity of these organizations has not been focused
on economic issues. They have, rather, been struggling over
issues of *control, self-determination* and *independence*: Shall
the poor have a voice in the allocation of War on Poverty
funds? Shall urban renewal be shaped by the people whose
neighborhood is being renewed? Shall the police be held accountable by the community? Who is to decide the dispensation of
welfare payments? Who makes the rules in the welfare bureaucracies? Who controls the ghetto?

The outcome of these grass-roots organizing efforts, of
course, cannot be predicted. The civil rights movements, in
its direct-action phase, began the process of bringing Negroes
and the poor into the political arena—and the results, in terms

of political alignments and issues, have already been substantial. The more recent efforts of political organization initiated by the participatory democrats will certainly increase the degree of Negro representation in the political process. These efforts are now being emulated by more established and less insurgent agencies—Martin Luther King's Southern Christian Leadership Conference, for example, in the massive organizing campaign in Chicago, used many of the techniques and rhetorical devices developed by SNCC and SDS.

It seems clear, then, that the poor are being organized and mobilized. But such mobilization can lead in two directions. On the one hand, there is the strong probability that the newly developed constituencies will take their place alongside other ethnic and interest groups, bargaining for benefits within the framework of the Democratic party. An alternative to this path is embodied in the vision of participatory democracy—the development of community-based, self-determining organizations, having the following functions:

> Achieving community control over previously centralized functions, through local election of school and police administrators; by forming community-run cooperatives in housing, social services, retail distribution and the like; by establishing community-run foundations and corporations.
> Maintaining close control over elected representatives; running and electing poor people to public office; ensuring direct participation of the community in framing political platforms and in shaping the behavior of representatives.
> Acting like a trade union in protecting the poor against exploitive and callous practices of public and private bureaucracies, landlords, businessmen, etc.

3. The values underlying participatory democracy have, so far, achieved their fullest expression in efforts to organize and mobilize communities of disenfranchised people, but such democratizing trends and potentialities also exist in other sectors of society. The most obvious example is the nationwide effort by university students to change the authority structure in American higher education. For the most part, this activity has been directed at protest against arbitrary restrictions of student political expression, and against paternalistic regulations limit-

ing students' rights to privacy and self-expression. The most dramatic and widely-known instance of this activity was that of the civil disobedience and student strikes at Berkeley in the fall of 1964. But the Berkeley situation has been repeated in less intense form on scores of campuses across the country. Student reform efforts have increasingly shifted from protest and direct action to demands for a continuing voice in the shaping of university policy. Some students now have demanded representation on administrative committees. Others have looked to the formation of organizations along the trade union model—organizations which would be independent of and could bargain with university administrators, rather than becoming participants in administration. Thus far, the impact of the student protest has been to generate a considerable degree of ferment, of re-examination and experimentation among college faculties and administrators, as well as efforts coercively to repress the protest.

Student protest has spread from the elite, liberal campuses to Catholic schools, and from there to other clerical bodies. The talk at Catholic seminaries now prominently includes "participatory democracy," and "New Left" clergymen have gone so far as to propose the establishment of a trade union for priests. But the University and the Church are not the only institutions witnessing challenges to existing authority structures. In recent years, there has been an enormous growth of unionization among schoolteachers and other white-collar workers, particularly among employees in the welfare bureaucracies. Now one can also observe ferment within the professions: young doctors and young lawyers are developing organizations dedicated to challenging the authority of the highly conservative professional societies, and to bringing an active sense of social responsibility to their professions.

It is not farfetched to predict that the idea of "Workers' control" will soon become a highly relevant issue in American life. American industrial unions have largely had to sacrifice the struggle for control in the work place for higher wages and fringe benefits; but at union conventions, control over working conditions is repeatedly urged as a high-priority bargaining demand. The impetus for making such a demand paramount, however, may first come from the ranks of white-collar and professional employees. The authority structure of the modern bureaucratic organization is plainly unsuited for a work force which is highly educated and fully aware of its competence to participate in decision-making. The first impulse of modern managers faced with threats to authority has been to make small concessions ("improve channels of communications"). But the exciting time will come when such insurgency turns from protest over small grievances to a full-fledged realization of the possibilities for first-class citizenship within public bureaucracies and private corporations. The forms of such democratization could include further unionization of the unorganized, worker representation in management, young-turk overthrows of entrenched leaderships in the professions, and, ultimately, demands for elections and recall of managers and administrators, and for employee participation in the shaping of policies and regulations.

4. The most authoritarian sector of public decision-making in the U.S. is in the area of foreign policy. The American Constitution gives enormous power to the President to make foreign policy without substantial built-in checks from Congress. The scope of Presidential power has, of course, been greatly expanded by the technology of modern war; the unchecked power of the government to mobilize support for its policies has been greatly enhanced by the invention of conscription, by the mass media and their centralization, by covert inteligence operations, etc. It is not surprising that foreign policy has been the special province of elites in America and, since World War II, has been carried on within a framework of almost total popular acquiescence.

The simultaneous occurrence of the Vietnam War and the emergence of a New Left in America may generate change in this situation. Due largely to student initiative, we are witnessing more protest during time of war than in any other comparable period in U.S. history. Not only does this protest begin to shatter the foreign policy consensus, but it also shows signs of bringing about more permanent change in the structure of foreign policy decision-making.

First, the teach-ins and similar initiatives mark the emergence of an *independent public* in the foreign policy area—a body of people, satisfied neither with official policy nor with official justifications of policy, determined to formulate alternatives, stimulate debate and criticism, and obtain independent sources of information. This public is to be found largely in universities but now spills over to include much of the intellectual community in the country. Moreover the teach-in as a technique for disseminating information suggests, at least symbolically, a significant breakthrough in the effort to find alternatives to the propaganda media controlled or manipulated by the state.

Second, the emerging foreign policy public has plainly had an at least transitory impact on Congress. The revival of Congressional independence with respect to foreign policy would be a signal advance of democracy in America.

Third, the attempts to find a non-religious moral ground for conscientious objection in time of war has led to a rediscovery of the Allied case at the Nuremberg Trials—a case which argued in essence that individuals were responsible for the actions of institutions taken in their name. This principle, taken seriously, is revolutionary in its implications for individual–state relations; and it converges, interestingly enough with "participatory democracy." The Nuremberg principle is now being used as a basis for legal defense of draft-refusal and civil disobedience at draft boards; it inspires professors to refuse to grade their students and become thereby accomplices to Selective Service; it inspires intellectuals and artists to acts of public defiance and witness. In fact, it is possible that one positive outcome of the war in Vietnam will have been its impact on the moral sensibility of many members of the intellectual and religious communities— forcing them to rethink their relationship to the state and to the institutions of war.

It is possible, then, that an unforeseen by-product of the highly-developed society is the emergence of potential publics that are (a) competent to evaluate the propaganda of elites (b) impatient with chauvinistic definitions of loyalty. The organization of such publics in the U.S. may be a significant outcome of the war in Vietnam. These publics do not have the power to change the course of this war, but the spread of their influence may be a factor in transforming the issues and alignments of American politics in the coming period. Moreover, the strength of these publics on the campus is now being reflected in the growing conflict over the role of the universities in national mobilization. The current campaign to prevent university participation in the Selective Service induction process may portend a more profound effort to make universities centers of resistance to encroaching militarization. The outcome of this particular struggle could be important in democratizing the structure of foreign policy decision-making.

5. The development of democratic consciousness in communities, organizations, and foreign policy decision-making will mean little if the national distribution of power remains undisturbed. This means that the social theory of the New Left must be centrally concerned with the development of relevant models for democratic control over public decisions at the national level.

It is clear that implicit in the New Left's vision is the notion that participatory democracy is not possible without some version of public control over the allocation of resources, economic planning, and the operation of large corporations. Such control is, of course, not missing in the United States. The federal government has taken responsibility for national planning to avoid slump, to control wages and prices, and to avoid inflation. Moreover, the postwar period has seen a tremendous increase in public subsidy of the corporate economy—through the defense budget, urban redevelopment, investment in research and education, transportation and communication, etc. In many ways the "two governments"—political and corporate—are merged, and this merger approximates an elitist corporatist model (hence breaking down even the modest pluralism which once characterized the system). The further development of this trend will foreclose any possibility for the achievement of democratic participation.

The demand for more national planning, once the major plank of American socialism, is now decidedly on the agenda of American political and corporate elites. The question for the Left has become how to *democratize* that planning. There are as yet no answers to this, or to the question of how to bring the large corporations under democratic control.

6. Thus the main intellectual problem for the new radicals is to suggest how patterns of decentralized decision-making in city administrations, and democratized authority structures in bureaucracies, can be meshed with a situation of greatly broadened national planning and coordination in the economy.

That no such programs and models now exist is, of course, a consequence of the disintegration of the socialist tradition in America and of the continuing fragmentation of American intellectual life. Unless the New Left consciously accepts the task of restoring that tradition and of establishing a new political community, the democratizing revolts which it now catalyzes are likely to be abortive.

7. These tasks were, less than a generation ago, declared by many American intellectuals to be no longer relevant. Ideology, it was argued, had no place in highly developed societies where problems of resource allocation had become technical matters. But the reverse may be true: that ideological questions—that is, questions about the structure and distribution of power—are *especially* pertinent when societies have the capacity to solve the merely technical problems.

It seems clear that the issue in a highly developed society is not simply economic exploitation; it is the question of the relationship of the individual to institutional and state authority which assumes paramount importance. In America, today, the familiar mechanisms of social control—money, status, patriotic and religious symbols—are losing their force for a population (particularly the new generation) which has learned to be intensely self-conscious and simultaneously worldly; to expect love and self-fulfillment; to quest for freedom and autonomy. All this learning is a consequence of increasingly sophisticated educational opportunities, of increasing liberated standards in family and interpersonal relations, of affluence itself. Against this learning, the classic patterns of elite rule, bureaucratic authority, managerial manipulation, and class domination will have a difficult time sustaining themselves.

The virtue of "participatory democracy," as a basis for a new politics, is that it enables these new sources of social tension to achieve political expression. Participatory democrocy symbolizes the restoration of personal freedom and interpersonal community as central political and social issues. It is not the end of ideology; it is a new beginning.

Marxism and the New Left

Howard Zinn

My intention in this paper is not to define the radicalism of the New Left but to redefine it. By a remarkable coincidence, that is, I believe, in the spirit of Marxism—to declare what something *is* by declaring what it should be—Marxism assumes that everything—including an idea—takes on a new meaning in each additional moment of time, in each unique historical situation. It tries to avoid academic scholasticism, which pretends to dutifully record, to describe—forgetting that to merely describe is to circumscribe. (The pretense of passive description is what Herbert Marcuse in *One-Dimensional Man* called *operationalism*.)

Marxism is not a fixed body of dogma, to be put into big black books or little red books, and memorized, but a set of specific propositions about the modern world which are both tough and tentative, plus a certain vague and yet exhilarating vision of the future, and, more fundamentally, an approach to life, to people, to ourselves, a certain way of thinking about thinking as well as about being. Most of all it is a way of thinking which is intended to promote action.

The New Left—that loose amalgam of civil rights activists, Black Power advocates, ghetto organizers, student rebels, Vietnam protestors—has been exciting because it has been acting. In that circle of encounter where the spirit of Marxism and the action of the New Left intersect, the New Left will take from Marxism—if it is wise—not all of its exact propositions about the world Marx and Engels lived in (a world which is partly the same today and partly different), but its approach. This approach demands a constant redefinition of theory in the light of immediate reality, and an insistence on *action* as a way of both testing and reworking theory.

---

* *Marxism and The New Left*, ed. Priscilla Long, p. 56–67, E. N. Sargent, Boston. Reprinted with permission.

One of the most quoted, and most ignored, in practice, of Marx's statements is the eleventh point of his *Theses on Feuerbach* (about 1945) : "The philosophers have only interpreted the world in various ways; the point however is to change it." Since any body of ideas is part of the world, this suggests our job is not merely to interpret Marxism and the New Left, but to change them. Earlier in these *Theses,* Marx criticized Feuerbach's emphasis on "the theoretical attitude." He said: "Social life is essentially practical. All mysteries . . . find their rational solution in human practice."

In their best moments, thinking revolutionaries agree with this. When Mao Tse Tung was in Yenan, after the Long March, he gave his lecture "On Practice," where he talked of the primacy of experience in knowledge, of uniting perceptual knowledge with rational knowledge, rationalism with empiricism. He said: "The Marxist recognizes that in the absolute, total process of the development of the universe, the development of each concrete process is relative; hence in the great stream of absolute truth, man's knowledge of the concrete process at each given stage of development is only relatively true." That spirit is somehow different than what one encounters in the *Peking Review* these days, with its litany: Long Live Chairman Mao.

To try for a moment to act out the Marxist approach: look at the academic setting in which we live. We find that so much of what is called "intellectual history" is the aimless dredging up of what is and was, rather than a creative recollection of experience pointed at the betterment of human life. We are surrounded by solemn, pretentious argument about what Marx or Machiavelli or Rousseau really meant about who was right and who was wrong—all of which is another way the pedant has of saying: "I am right and you are wrong." Too much of what passes for the theoretical discussion of public issues is really a personal duel for honor or privilege—with each discussant like the character in *Catch-22* who saw every event in the world as either a feather in his cap or a black eye—and this while men were dying all around him.

This scholasticism, oddly enough, has been typical both of the Old Left and of the academic journals, journals which would be horrified at being called Left or Right, and which indeed could hardly be accused of moving in any identifiable direction. Because the New Left is a successor to the Old Left in American history, and because it comes to a large extent out of the academic world (whether the Negro colleges of the South or the Berkeleys of the North), it is always being tempted by theoretical irrelevancies. Fortunately, the young people of today seem more nimble than their predecessors in avoiding this trap.

The contributions of the Old Left—and they were considerable—came not out of its ideological fetishism but out of its action. What gave it dynamism was not the classes on surplus value but the organization of the CIO, not the analysis of Stalin's views on the National and Colonial Question, but the fight for the Scottsboro boys, not the labored rationale for dictatorship of the proletariat, but the sacrifices of the Abraham Lincoln Battalion. I am not arguing here against theoretical discussion, or against long-range principles, or the analysis of sub-surface realities, but I am asserting that theory must be informed by observation and expressed in action. It must, in other words, be relevant.

A materialist approach—in the Marxian sense—makes suggestions rather than demands. One of these is that we look for the situational circumstances behind the behavior and thought of of men, if we want to affect both. A dialectical approach—in the Marxian sense—suggests that we evaluate a situation not as fixed, but as in motion, and that our evaluation itself affects that motion. Dialectical materialism asks awareness that we are creatures of limited vision, in eyes and brain, and so must not assume that what we see or perceive is all—that conflicting tendencies often lie beneath the surface of any event.

These are not just academic observations: such an approach should make it easier for us to understand what is wrong when the government says to a penniless Negro in the Mississippi Delta, we have passed a bill and you are now free. Such an approach should help us to sense, in walking past the tenements of a city, temporarily quiet, the element of a violent insurrection. Marx's emphasis on the tyranny of economics can't tell us *how much* economic motivation there is behind any specific political act, but it can lead us to look for it. And so the New Left might go overboard in stressing economic interests in Southeast Asia as an explanation for escalation in Vietnam—but it might be devilishly right in noting the connection between U.S. economic interests in Latin American nations and the pro-American votes of these nations in the U.N.

Marxism, in other words, doesn't tell us *exactly* what we will find beneath the surface—it does suggest what we should look for —and it certainly insists that we look. A Marxist would have given Lysenko his microscope; but it was a Stalinist who told him—or created an atmosphere that told him—what he must find beneath it.

And if someone says this isn't dialectical materialism or Marxism—this is common sense, or rationalism, or pragmatism, or empiricism, or naturalism—why deny that, or argue? Who cares about credit? True, the Old Left didn't like to admit relations with any other ideology. It remained virginal and lonely. The New Left seems different.

There has been much talk about a Christian-Marxist dialogue—but if such a dialogue is to be useful perhaps it should begin with the idea that God is dead and Marx is dead, but Yossarian lives. This is only a way of saying: let's not spend our time arguing whether God exists or what Marx really meant, because while we argue, the world moves, while we publish, others perish, and the best use of our energy is to resist those who would send us—after so many missions of murder—on still one more.

A new radicalism should be anti-ideological, I believe, in the sense I have discussed. But it also should be—and here it has been inadequate—concerned with theory. I see three essential ingredients in such a theory. First we need a vision of what we are working toward—one based on transcendental human needs and not limited by the reality we are so far stuck with. Second, this theory should analyze the present reality, not through the prism of old, fixed categories, but rather with an awareness of the unique here and now of the need to make the present irrationality intelligible to those around us. Finally, such a theory would explore—in the midst of action—effective techniques of social change for the particular circumstances we find at the moment.

Let me speak now about the first requirement of this theory, the vision of the future. Here the Marxian vision is useful. True, it is vague. But what better guard is there against dogmatism than vagueness? Uncertainty is not a virtue in depicting the facts of the moment; it may not only be tolerable, but desirable, in trying to portray the future.

I stress this as a Marxian vision, even though many non-Marxists have held the same vision—because while it's necessary to emphasize to the Left that it does not monopolize either compassion or insight, it is necessary to remind everyone else—the Christians, the Jews, the Buddhists, the Humanists, and anyone else—that they share certain aims with Marxism. No one of these groups is going to revolutionize the world by itself, and so all need to be reminded of a certain consensus of humanistic values that has developed in the modern world. Marxists and liberals at their best (and they have not usually been at their best) share this theoretical consensus, here and abroad. Indeed, one of the great contributions of the New Left has been to remind both Marxist countries and liberal capitalist countries how far is their behavior from the values they claim.

In *The Holy Family*, one of the early writings of Marx and Engels (about 1845) they say man needs to be "not negatively free to avoid this or that event" but "positively free to express his true individuality." They say this requires arranging the empirical world around us so that "man experiences and assimilates there what is really human, that he experiences himself as a man." Rather than punishing individuals for their crimes, we should "destroy the social conditions which engender crime, and give to each individual the scope which he needs in society in order to develop his life." This speaks to the co-called socialist countries of today which imprison writers who criticize the state. It also speaks to a country like the United States, which gives people the negative freedoms of the Bill of Rights, but distributes very unequally the scope in which people can develop their individuality, can exercise their freedom—so that some children can roam in little suburban mansions surrounded by gardens, and others are equally free to play in rat-infested tenements. While every one "has" freedom of speech, the corporation with a million dollars to spend on television time can speak to thirty million people, and the individual who can afford a soap box can speak to thirty people. What makes the New Left so critical of the wealthiest nation in the world is its acute consciousness that freedom means not only legal permission to occupy space, but the resources to make the most of this.

The New Left has not even begun to figure out how to explain this complex problem of freedom to all those people in the United States brought up on high school history books and American Legion essay contests. What can make the New Radicalism really new, and really pertinent to here and now, is to be able, without recourse to the state slogans about "bourgeois freedom," to do justice to the degree of freedom that does exist for people in the United States—while noting that it *is* a matter of degree, that freedom in America is like wealth, plentiful, and very unequally distributed.

Let me turn to another element in the Marxian vision. There is still a widespread popular belief, heavily stressed on the *Reader's Digest* level that Marxism believes in the supremacy of the state over the individual, while democracy believes the opposite. In fact, the existence of oppressively overbearing states in the world, which call themselves Marxist, reinforces this idea. But a true radicalism would remind people in both socialist and capitalist countries of Marx's and Engels' hope, expressed early in the *Manifesto,* that some day "the public power will lose its political character" and "we shall have an association in which the free development of each is the condition for the free development of all." This is not just a youthful aberration (there is a fad about the young romantic Marx and the old, practical Marx) because twenty-seven years later, Marx, in his *Critique of the Gotha Program,* says: "Freedom consists in converting the state from an organ superimposed upon society into one completely subordinate to it." Here also he says, on the subject of the state giving education to the people, "the state has need, on the contrary, of a very stern education by the people." And Engels, a year after Marx's death, in 1884, writes in his *Origin of the Family, Private Property and the State:*

> The society that will organize production on the basis of a free and equal association of the producers will put the whole machinery of state where it will then belong: into the museum of antiquities, by the side of the spinning wheel and the bronze ax.

Their attitude to the state is made even clearer and more specific in Marx's book on the *Civil War in France,* and Engels' *Introduction* to it, where, both of them point admiringly to the Paris Commune of early 1871. The Commune almost immediately abolished conscription and the standing army, declared universal suffrage and the right of citizens to recall their elected officials at any time, said all officials, high or low, should be paid the same wage as received by other workers, and publicly burned the guillotine.

The New Left is anti-authoritarian; it would—I expect—burn draft cards in any society. It is anarchistic not just in wanting the ultimate abolition of the state, but in its immediate requirement that authority and coercion be banished in every sphere of existence, that the end must be represented immediately in the means. Marx and Bakunin disagreed on this, but the New Left has the advantage over Marx of having an extra century of history to study. We see how a dictatorship of the proletariat can easily become a dictatorship over the proletariat, as Trotsky warned, as Rosa Luxemburg warned. The New Left should remind the socialist states as well as the capitalist states of Marx's letter of 1853 to the *New York Tribune* saying he didn't know how capital punishment could be justified "in a society glorying in its civilization."

In America, both liberalism and radicalism were beguiled into cheering for state power because under F.D.R. it seemed beneficent: it enacted certain economic reforms, and it waged war against Hitler. The New Left, hopefully, will recognize that the state cannot be trusted, either to carry reforms far enough, or to drop bombs only on Nazi invaders and not on Asian peasants in their own country. It will therefore create constellations of power outside the state to pressure it into humane actions, to resist its inhumane actions, and to replace it in many functions by voluntary small groups seeking to maintain both individuality and co-operation. Black Power, in its best aspects, is such an endeavor.

The New Left in America needs to show people how the state, whether a proletarian dictatorship or a sophisticated welfare capitalism, constitutes a special interest of its own which deserves not unthinking loyalty, but criticism, resistance, and (even in its better moments) watchfulness. This New Left attitude toward the state expresses a more general attitude—against making instruments into absolutes or means into ends—against the deification of any party, any nation, any ideology, any method.

Now another point about the Marxian vision. Perhaps nowhere does Marx speak more directly to our mass society today, and therefore to the new radicals in mass society, than in his *Economic and Philosophical Manuscripts* of 1944. The estrangement of man described there is pertinent not only to the classical proletariat of his time but to all classes in every modern industrial society—and certainly to the young people of this generation in the United States. He talks of men producing things alien to themselves, which become monsters independent of them (look all around us, at our automobiles, our television sets, our skyscrapers, even our universities). People find no satisfaction in working. He points to the irony that in man's specifically human functions (working, creating) he feels like an animal, while only in his animal functions (eating, sex) does he feel like a human being. Our activity becomes not enjoyable in itself, but just a means to keep alive. Activity *is* life—what else is life?—and yet it becomes in modern society only a means to life.

So, we become estranged from what we produce, from our own activity, from our fellow men, from nature (here Marxism must share credit with Taoism), and finally from ourselves—because we all find ourselves living another life, not the one we really want to live. The new radicals of today are desperately conscious of this and try to escape it. They want to do work which is congenial to them—so they go to Mississippi or move into the ghetto—or they don't work at all rather than work at hateful or parasitic jobs. They often try to create relationships with one another which are not warped by the rules and demands of the world around them. The crucial cause of all these forms of estrangement is that people's activities are coerced rather than free, and so the young people today are defiant. This is not easy, but the very act of attempting it is a free act.

From all this it is quite clear what Marx's values were; the free man, in his individuality, in his sociality, in his oneness with nature. The New Left is in accord here. Where it parts, I think, is in Marx's claim—although some attribute this to Engels (one of those academic disputes I spoke about) that this version of unalienated man springs not from a wish, but from an observation—from a scientific plotting of a historical curve which moves inevitably in the direction of man's freedom.

Surely we don't have such confidence in inevitabilities these days—we've had too many surprises in this century. (Simone de Beauvoir says in her book *The Ethics of Antiquity* that there is no inevitable proletarian uprising—the movement may go in six different directions.) We are unabashed in declaring our subjective wants and desires—without needing a "scientific" basis for such wants. Here again, the discussion of whether ethical norms are grounded in empirical science is one of those academic discussions which lead us nowhere in actuality. Surely, most people agree on the gross necessities of life—food, sex, peace, freedom, love, dignity, self-realization. Our energy should be spent in working toward them, not in discussing their metaphysical meaning.

I suggested above that the second requirement of a pertinent theory is an analysis of the *particulars* of today's reality. One of Marx's great perceptions was that there is a material basis for man's alienation and unhappiness—the scarcity of goods which he and society need, producing conflict, exploitation, coercion. Thus, abundance is a prerequisite—though not a guarantee—of man's freedom. In the United States, we face this paradox, that the state with the most enormous productive apparatus, indeed the only state in the world which has the technological capacity to have communism, and where a communist society would have the greatest chance of preserving the freedom of the individual (because the *socialist* societies are plagued by scarcity) gets apoplectic at the very mention of the word.

It is here in the United States that the slogan "to each according to his need" can have meaning. We have enough doctors and hospitals to give adequate medical care to whoever needs it, without rationing this according to wealth. We grow enough food in this country without insisting that people without money do with very little food. We can—if we want to—build enough homes in this country to eliminate slums. And so on. There is room for some scholarly work here: economists could sit down somewhere and work out a specific plan for free food in America, also for free college tuition and allowances. What the New Left needs to show, and in specific detail, is where the resources are in this country, what they *are* being used for, and what they *could* be used for.

The Marxian economic categories have long provided material for academic controversy—and I doubt that Marx intended this. But he was only human and perhaps he too succumbed to the temptations of the intellectual: his research, his curiosity, his passion for scheme-building and for scientific constructions ran away with him. I confess that I cannot see how his dense Volume II of *Das Kapital* on the "Circulation of Commodities" or his long expositions of absolute rent and differential rent are essential to revolutionary theory. Does it really matter if Böhm-Bawerk was right or wrong on the relationship between aggregate surplus value and aggregate prices of production?

Even so brilliant a theory as that of surplus-value—how relevant is it to social action? Has the militancy of workingmen in history required such an analysis to sustain it? Has such militancy been transformed into revolutionary consciousness anywhere by the comprehension of the distinction between the use value and exchange value of labor power? The Baran-Sweezy notion of a surplus (in *Monopoly Capital*) comprised of waste, military expenses, and unused capacity, is more fruitful, I think, as a theoretical prod to revolutionary action.

James Bevel is right when he says you can only organize large numbers of people around issues that are obvious or that can easily be made obvious. So instead of discussing the falling rate of profit, or the organic composition of capital, I would concentrate on what is readily observable—that this country has enormous resources which it wastes shamefully and distributes unjustly. A country that produces 200 billion dollars worth of goods and services a year, and this is not our full capacity, should not have ten million families living below the $3000 a year level. All the Chamber of Commerce pronouncements, the fancy *Fortune Magazine* charts about our progress, the confident State of the Union Addresses fall apart when you take a long walk through any major American city: through Harlem or Roxbury or Chicago's South Side.

The most useful Marxian statement about capitalist society is the largest one—that in an era when production is a complex, world-wide social process, and requires rationality, our system is incredibly irrational. This is because corporate profit, not human need, governs what is produced and what is not produced. It is also because there is a huge vested interest—economic, military, political, psychological—in the production of present and future corpses, on which we spend seventy billion dollars a year. We spend about twenty billion dollars a year on public relations, advertising, promotion. We build too many cars, too many highways, too many office buildings, produce too many cigarettes, too much liquor, too many gadgets and not enough homes, schools, hospitals. Corporate profits after taxes amount to forty billion dollars a year—enough to raise every $3000 a year family to $7000 a year. The New Left, instead of getting involved in theoretical discussions about economic categories, needs to find ways to make clear to Americans how wasteful, irrational, and unjust is our economy.

With a vision of how man should live, and some perception of how men do live (and so many of us need to be *shown*), the most urgent theoretical problem for the New Left—and the one where traditional Marxism gives the least guidance—is: how do we change society? How do we redistribute the power in society in order to redistribute the wealth? How do we overcome those who are enjoying power and wealth and won't give it up? How do we stop the fanaticism of both civilian and military leaders who feel it is America's duty to establish its power, or its puppets, wherever possible in the world—and don't care how many people, Americans or others—they kill in the process?

The traditional Marxian idea of a revolution taking place because of a breakdown in the capitalist mechanism and an organized, class-conscious proletariat taking over, is hardly tenable today. Where socialist revolutions have taken place in the world, they have taken place mostly because war has weakened or destroyed the state and created a vacuum in which organized revolutionaries could take over. The traditional liberal idea of a gradual evolution towards freedom, peace, and democracy through parliamentary reform is also hardly tenable. We see that poverty and racism can be institutionalized, with only token steps taken to assuage their worst aspects; that by creating a contented, bloated middle class, by introducing state regulatory mechanisms in the economy, the staus quo can be maintained. And furthermore, in foreign policy, it has become accepted that the President and a small group of advisers make foreign policy, while the mass communications industry creates a nation of sheep who give assent.

Certainly, in the United States, the traditional idea that the agent of social change will be the proletariat needs re-examination, when the best-organized of the workers are bribed into silence with suburban houses and automobiles, and drugged into compliance with mass entertainment. Perhaps unorganized workers—the bulk of the labor force—may play a part, but these consist of white collar workers, domestic workers, migratory and farm laborers, service industry workers, and various kinds of people who are the hardest to organize. Recent experience suggests that Negroes—and perhaps Negroes in the ghetto—may be the most powerful single force for social change in the United States. Marx envisioned the industrial proletariat as the revolutionary agent because it was in need, exploited, and brought face to face in the factory. The Negro is in need, exploited and brought together in the ghetto. And since Berkeley and the teach-ins, there is some evidence that students—especially as they are pushed more and more toward the mouth of the cannon—may be another important agent of change. Perhaps some peculiar combination, unpredictable at this moment, will be formed in a time of national crisis.

How will change come about? By tactics short of violent revolution, but far more militant than normal parliamentary procedure, it seems to me. Even the demonstrations of the civil rights movement were not enough to achieve more than tokens of change: a few laws, a few high appointments, and LBJ reciting "We Shall Overcome." Spontaneous uprisings in the ghetto are alarm signals, but do not produce change in themselves. It will take systematic, persistent organizing and education, in the ghettos, in the universities, plus co-ordinated actions of various kinds to shock society out of its lethargy.

The New Left's idea of parallel organizations, as a way of *demonstrating* what people should do, how people should live, has enormous possibilities: freedom schools, free universities, free cities—remember how these grew up in medieval times outside the feudal system—self-controlled communities. But also, free, active *pockets* of people inside the traditional cities, universities, corporations. In military combat, guerrilla warfare arose as an answer to overwhelmingly centralized military power. Perhaps we are in need of political guerrilla tactics in the face of mass society—in which enclaves of freedom are created here and there in the midst of the orthodox way of life, to become centers of protest, and examples to other. It is in techniques of organization, pressure, change, community-building—that the New Radicals need the most thought, and the most action. It may take an ingenious combination of energy and wit to carry through a new kind of revolution.

Action *is* preferably organized, thought-out action, but there should be room for whatever kinds of action any individual or group feels moved to undertake. In an era when it is so easy to feel helpless, we need the Existentialist emphasis on our freedom to act. The Marxist-Existentialist debate on freedom and determinism seems to me to be an empty one—an academic one. To stress our freedom is not the result of ignorance that we do have a history, that we do have an oppressive environment. But knowing of these pressures on us, we should be existentially aware that there is enormous indeterminacy in the combat between us and the obstacles all around. We never know exactly the debt or the shallowness of the resistance to our actions— until we act. We never know exactly what effect we will have. Our actions may lead to nothing except changing ourselves, and that is something. They may have a tiny cumulative effect, along with a thousand other actions. They may also explode.

Chapter Two

Forms of Action: General Discussion

There exists, perhaps, no better discussion of the problem of action within the framework of a democratic society than Arthur Waskow's treatment of "creative disorder." Though written in response to the tactics of direct action used by the early Civil Rights Movement, it speaks directly to the legitimacy of New Left political activity. Waskow shares the view of Thomas Jefferson that history is not on the side of democratic institutions. Those institutions which once accommodated a democracy or, democratic republic, age and are no longer responsive to the changing needs of the people.

In order to safeguard the securities of a democracy in such a situation, it becomes necessary for new forms of popular expression to be created. These forms may at first be perceived as unlawful disruption of the normal political process, but in time they may be accepted as legitimate. Waskow argues that a truly vital citizenry always seeks to invent new forms of democratic action.

The Meaning of Creative Disorder*

Arthur Waskow

American society in the 1960s had such difficulty in coping with the concept of a whole range of politics lying between order and violence that it could find no single separate word for this sort of politics, and instead fell back on a negative definition by calling it "disorder" or "non-violence." We have here preferred the term "disorder" because much of the creative disorder in racial conflict of the 1960s was not "non-violent" in the pure Gandhian sense with which that word was often used. As we have used the term "disorder" here, it describes only behavior that is not violent in deed. But "non-violence," exemplified in the racial crisis of the 1960s by the work of Martin Luther King, came to mean specifically the Gandhian politics of love, the confrontation of conscience, and conversion through example and dignity.

Much of the civil rights movement of the 1960s was carried on according to King's and Gandhi's standards, but by no means all. Much of the politics of racial disorder had little to do with love or the confrontation of conscience—but equally little to do with outright violence. By Gandhi's standards, one should hate the oppressive system but love the oppressor himself as a human being; in a great deal of disorderly politics, young Negroes expressed intense anger and hatred not only for the segregation system but for the segregationists themselves or even for all whites. And yet this hatred was expressed by pursuing change, not by attacking the enemy; it was often pursued with no outright act of violence, though often with a "violent" heart and mind. What might be called the "not-quite-violent" and the "non-violent" approaches both, therefore, make up what we have here called the politics of disorder.

But there is a still deeper problem in the assessment of

---

* *From Race Riot to Sit-In*, 276–290, Doubleday New York. Reprinted with permission.

"disorder" as a form of politics: the difficulty in distinguishing it, in actual practice, from the politics of order and violence. For example, the efforts by SNCC to get Negro voters registered in Albany, Georgia—seemingly a thoroughly "orderly" notion that fit into traditional election politics—were closely connected with street marches for equal access to public accommodations and economic boycotts against discriminatory employers—and these marches and boycotts were unconventional and sometimes "disorderly" techniques. In such a case, it may not be easy to disentangle the politics of disorder from the politics of order. Again, after some mass public demonstrations by Negroes in some southern cities met with brutal violence from white mobs, some Negroes outside the official civil rights movement responded with street violence of their own. In such a case, it is not easy to disentangle the politics of disorder from the politics of violence.

Yet there seem to be some crucial differences, which perhaps can be expressed this way: All three forms of politics as used by the civil rights movement were concerned with bringing about change. But there was a difference in the extent to which people using the different forms tended to focus on the changes to be achieved, to the exclusion of focusing on the rules of the system that was to be changed or on those who defended that system. In the politics of order, people divide their attention between the changes to be accomplished and the accepted rules of society about the "legitimate" ways of bringing about change. In the politics of violence, people divide their attention between the changes to be accomplished and those powerful people who get in the way of change—the enemy. In the politics of disorder, people tend to reduce greatly their interest in both the given rules and the enemy; instead they focus very strongly on the changes to be accomplished. To oversimplify a bit: in the politics of order, men follow the rules; in the politics of violence, they attack their enemy; in the politics of disorder, they pursue change.

It can be argued that the civil rights movement of the 1960s actually accomplished more change in race relations than did either the politics of violence in 1919, 1943, and since, or the politics of order in 1866 and 1875 (the years of the first civil rights acts) and 1954 (the year of the Supreme Court's school desegregation decision). If so, the reason may well be that in focusing on the achievement of change rather than on the rules or the enemy, "disorder" in the racial struggle has actually brought about more change.

To the degree that the politics of disorder is aimed at bringing about change, it is generally invented by people who are "outside" a particular system of political order, and want to bring change about so that they can enter. In doing so, they tend to use new techniques that make sense to themselves out of their own experience, but that look disorderly to people who are thinking and acting inside the system. The Negroes were by no means the first to initiate this process. For example, in the seventeenth and eighteenth centuries, urban lawyers and merchants who could not get the entrenched politicians to pay attention to their grievances (and who were scarcely represented in Parliament) used the illegal and disorderly device of political pamphleteering against the established order. In the same way, nineteenth-century workers who could not get their employers or the elected legislators to pay attention to their demands used unionization and the strike—which at first were illegal—to call attention to their grievances. In both these cases, using the politics of disorder not only got the users accepted into the political order and got their immediate grievances looked after, but also got the new techniques accepted into the array of authorized and approved political methods. In short, the system of "order" was itself changed. Thus the "criminal libel" of political pamphleteering was enshrined as freedom of the press, and the "criminal conspiracy" of striking was enshrined in the system of free labor unions. One century's disorder became the next century's liberty under ordered law. Whether this will occur with the forms of creative disorder used by Negro Americans in their movement for racial equality has yet to be decided; but there are many indications that the process has begun.

Although we have focused upon the invention and use of "disorderly" techniques by racial equalitarians in the 1960s, these techniques have also been used by supporters of racial hierarchy and segregation. When the segregationists believed themselves to be the "outsiders," they turned to techniques not usually considered legitimate in the normal political order. For example, when segregationist Mississippians feared that federal marshals might try to arrest Governor Ross Barnett for contempt of a court order desegregating the University of Mississippi, thousands of them sat down around the governor's mansion to interpose their bodies—perhaps intending a "not-quite-violent" resistance—between him and the forces of law and order. Similarly, in parts of the South segregationists have used pressures analogous to the Negroes' economic boycott, as when they cut off bank credit or refused to sell tools and evicted tenants who tried to register to vote. In some northern cities, white parents have picketed school boards that tried to end *de facto* segregation in the schools, and in New York City especially, parents who opposed measures taken to desegregate "neighborhood" schools imitated the whole system of short-term boycotts of the public schools and the creation of short-term private protest schools that the Negroes had previously used.

The seeming paradox that both racial equalitarians and racial hierarchists could on occasion believe themselves "outside" the legitimate political order and therefore forced to use "disorderly" forms of politics is in reality no paradox at all. During the 1960s one of these groups which had long been securely within the political order—the hierarchists and segregationists—was slowly being pushed outside it. At the same time, the equalitarians and integrationists, or at least the bulk of the Negroes among them, who had long been excluded from the political order, were slowly being included for the first time. During the transition period, both groups had reason to feel like "outsiders" and to use the methods of disorder.

During this period of sustained disorder from both sides in the racial conflict, the federal government moved further than it had during the brief period of violence in 1919 toward acting like a "state." Because both of those groups using the politics of disorder were so powerful and because opinion in the society at large remained so deeply divided over the values of racial hierarchy as against racial equality, during the early 1960s there was strong pressure on practically all American political institutions to tolerate disorder when used by either side on the racial question, so long as violence was avoided; to prevent, halt, and punish violence by either side; and to draw back from what would have been a truly "governmental" act, the police enforcement of either side's view of the race question. Even then, there was difficulty in bringing an American "state" on the race question to full fruition. Attorney-General Kennedy's difficulty in distinguishing a "state" from a "government," as when he opposed the original Title III of the civil rights bill for fear that a "national police force" could not simply prevent violence but would have to conquer the South, was one measure of the difficulty. But the growing strength of the "state" position can be seen from the desire of congressmen to enact Title III and from the position taken by the Justice Department in its *amicus* brief for the Supreme Court on the sit-in cases.

In both of these instances, unlikely organs of government were defending the notion that federal power should be exterted to protect disorder without violence. Obviously, neither the Justice Department nor members of Congress came easily to the position that the protection of disorder was more desirable than the establishment of a new order; their institutional roles require both of them to fear disorder and insist on the value of order. But because of the depth and intensity of the conflict over racial equality or hierarchy, both came to believe that an attempt to impose order might result instead in violence, and disorder should therefore be permitted and protected so long as it did not become violence. The transformation of disorder into order would have to await the creation of a much broader agreement on which "order" should be upheld.

As for the "church" aspects of federal authority, it could be argued that the 1954 Supreme Court decision on school desegregation was the crucial event in beginning to establish official values based on racial equality. Although in several instances direct violations of court orders for school desegregation were confronted by federal enforcement of the orders, the court decision had far more impact in the realm of values and morality —for example, in raising the expectations of young Negroes that finally erupted in the sit-ins—than it did in establishing directly enforceable law. And it is important to note that despite its high permanent prestige as an American "church," the Supreme Court from almost the moment of its decision began to suffer vigorous attacks, which demonstrated the absence of any real national consensus and the resistance to any single national "church" on the race question.

It was not really until the Civil Rights Act of 1964 was passed that the aspects of the "state" on racial issues that the Federal government had begun to take on in response to the 1919 riots and the aspects of the "church" on racial issues that it had begun to take on in 1954 were merged effectively into new law. Thus not until 1964 can there be said to have emerged the beginnings of an American "government" on the race question.[1]

What is likely to happen to that "government," barely born in 1964, and what may happen to the politics of order, disorder, and violence as they have been used in the racial conflict? To the extent that the Civil Rights Act of 1964 created a "government" on the race question, it is only a weak and tentative government. As the Negroes of Mississippi and Harlem—more generally speaking, the Deep South, most rural and most repressive, and the Deep North, most urban and most desperate —made clear as soon as the act was passed, it did not meet their problems. It would take new acts of "government" to bring Harlem and Mississippi fully into the American political system. And if the past is any indication of the future, such acts of new "government" are more likely to occur if they have been demanded by those who are still outside the political system, through acts of creative disorder.

What then is likely to be the future of the politics of disorder within the movement for racial equality? Will the new political forms wither away if equalitarians win more and more victories, or will the techniques outlive the particular issues? Which of the techniques are likely to prove most effective and creative? Is disorder often likely to escalate from the boycott or the sit-in to full-scale social disruption, or will the hostility to this form of attack prevent its being often used?

The answers to these questions will depend mostly upon two factors: the response of political authorities to the use of controlled forms of disorder as ways of attracting public attention to and bringing about a resolution of particular conflicts; and the degree of inventiveness and self-discipline in the Negro

---

[1] An abortive effort at creating a true federal "government" on the race question was made during Reconstruction, but soon failed.

community as it tries to create new techniques to cope with whatever failures may occur in the use of controlled disorder.

As to the political authorities: if the local police try to smash equivalents of a "riot" that use no violence, they are much more likely to find real riots blossoming before them, or perhaps efforts at general social disruption. Even if the police attack not the organized, deliberate equalitarian movements that are using creative disorder (as the police more frequently do in the South) but instead a number of unorganized, individual, "troublesome" Negroes (as they more frequently do in the North), they may find the Negro community ready to boil over into riots. If, on the other hand, all the governments concerned, local and national, step back and allow sit-ins, boycotts, and rent strikes to be "fought out" just as most labor strikes and lock-outs are, so long as neither side uses violence, and if local and national authorities act to punish violence used by either side in the racial conflict, then it is unlikely that efforts at creative disorder will degenerate into rioting. But a movement in this direction would require from the federal government the imagination necessary to build the kind of federal police force that could check and prevent particular acts of violence against Negroes, even violence by local police, without taking over entire cities and states.

It is not only deliberate police action to smash controlled creative disorder that may result in its degeneration into violence or disruption. If political authorities simply ignore attempts to use controlled disorder, its users may try the more threatening techniques. Limited forms of disorder seem less able to attract attention and disturb the authorities in a great and complex northern metropolis than in a middle-sized southern town or the rural Black Belt. Frustrated protestants in the northern cities who see their efforts at controlled disorder going for nought might well keep on trying such generally disruptive techniques as the World's Fair stall-in or blocking New York's Triborough Bridge, especially since the greater complexity of metropolitan society is likely to make it more vulnerable to small but carefully chosen acts of social disruption. Or if the failure of controlled creative disorder disillusions and discourages large numbers of urban Negroes, they may become ready tinder for a spark of riot. On the other hand, forms of limited disorder might become accepted throughout the United States as reasonable methods for persuading legislators and officials to change their minds—akin to free speech, in other words. If this is the direction of change—if the Congress and local governments fully accept sit-ins, marches, boycotts, and rent strikes as legitimate expressions of public desires and change their behavior accordingly—then it is rather unlikely that disorder will escalate into efforts at social disruption, or into rioting.

As to the degree of inventiveness in the Negro community: The question will be whether there is in existence a leadership that is committed to avoiding violence, that is capable of creating new forms of disorder without violence, and that can keep in close touch with its constituents in the Negro population. If so, the chances for riot would decrease, as compared to the chances of new forms of disorder. So far, Negro leaders in the North seem to have had difficulty in inventing new forms of disorder that would appeal to one specific and extremely important group: adolescent youths and young men without jobs or education. The southern sit-ins and marches have evidently appealed to some of the same qualities of masculinity and physical courage that make many young men good soldiers. But the northern rent strike and economic boycott seemed to appeal to or be activities more easily carried out by quieter, older people. Although school boycotts and job blockades may appeal to the young, they cannot easily involve those who have already quit school or those who do not have the skills necessary to hold existing jobs; and it is exactly these men who are most likely to resort to violence. In the absence of new inventions in creative disorder that appeal to young men in the North, therefore, riots there may become more likely.[2]

Such new inventions would not only have to appeal to the young, but show hope of dealing with the deeper diseases of life in the great northern metropolises. Thus they would have to be directed at increasing the total number of jobs, and perhaps at

---

[2] These words were written before, and seem partially confirmed by, the Los Angeles race riot of September 12–16, 1965. In the area of heaviest rioting, unemployment levels among young men were especially high, action under the official poverty program had been stymied by the refusal of local authorities to accept major involvement of the poor in determination of their own needs and goals, and unofficial institutions that might have energized

getting new sorts of activity that did not utilize presently recognized skills accepted into the arena of paid employment—rather than at merely getting more Negroes into the present jobs. They would have to be aimed at improving the schools and perhaps at changing the kinds of schools made available—rather than at merely trying to integrate the present schools. Similarly with housing, the welfare system, and other aspects of metropolitan

---

the poor into non-violent action and protest (such as SNCC or CORE) had made few efforts to activate the area, partly for lack of ideas as to how to focus non-violent action around the real needs of people in the area. As for the indigenous invention of non-violent protest by residents of the riot area, the only evidence of indigenous organization is the report that a "War Council" of young men formed after the first day of the riot to manage continued attacks and distribute assignments. Its focus at that time was clearly on the politics of violence, not of creative disorder; but its emergence may offer a starting point for future efforts to encourage the development of creative-disorder protests in Los Angeles.

In light of the theory of riots that has been sketched above, particularly in Chapter X, it is interesting to note the riot was triggered by an incident involving the arrest of a Negro by a white policeman, and fed upon the belief, widely and strongly held by Negroes in the area, that the Los Angeles police were bitterly anti-Negro in deed as well as word. This belief may well have been reinforced during the riot itself by the tenor of the statements made by Chief of Police William H. Parker in constantly repeated television appearances. There is some slight evidence that the intervention of the California National Guard may have helped reduce the violence because the Guard did not have an established anti-Negro reputation. But the anti-police aspects of the riot, especially when added to those apparent in the Harlem, Philadelphia, and Rochester riots of 1964, suggest that measures to ensure the neutrality of the police on racial questions may have to go beyond the creation of civilian review boards and similar devices. For example, the legitimacy of the police might conceivably be strengthened in large cities by making subdivisions of the police force in some measure responsible to neighborhoods or large sections of the city—through area-wide election of division police chiefs, for example, or even of policemen on the beat, on the same principle as the election of sheriffs in rural America.

[3] One proposed form of creative disorder that might meet these criteria is that of Paul Jacobs for a "work-in," in which unemployed whites and Negroes might learn the medium-level skills necessary for jobs that need doing but are unfilled or do not exist (such as assistant nurses and assistant teachers), and simply show up to do such jobs, risking arrest if necessary in order to persevere at the work-in until their new jobs were recognized and paid for. This would reverse the symbolism of the job blockade, which tries to prevent others from working.

life. Since most of these issues are decided not by private interests chiefly but by the local and federal governments, such new forms of disorder might have to confront particular agencies of government without posing a disruptive or "insurrectionary" threat to the social system or government as a whole.[3]

The two sets of changes that from the discussion above seem to be necessary if violence and social disruption are to be avoided can be summed up as, first, the bringing to fruition of an American "state" on racial questions; and second, the invention and legitimation of a number of new techniques of controlled creative disorder. The first of these means that some form of federal police force must be created to prevent violence from being used by either side in the racial conflict, including violence that takes on the color of legitimacy because it is carried on by local police who are in fact merely acting on behalf of one side or the other. Such a force would have to be carefully aimed at the protection of creative disorder used by either side in the racial conflict, and would have to be carefully restricted from itself defending one view or the other of racial justice. Indeed, it would probably be wise to set up a separate force for this purpose, so as to avoid involving those enforcement officers who carry out "governmental" mandates to the degree that they exist on the racial issue —for example, the public accommodations provisions of the Civil Rights Act of 1964.[4]

Conceivably, such a force might be most effective if there were also created a system for managing and coping with particular disorderly techniques used in racial conflict, just as the Wagner Labor Relations Act created ways of recognizing certain agents of labor and management as legitimate conflict organizations, approving some forms of labor-management disorder, ruling others out of bounds, and encouraging bargaining between the parties. If American society were to achieve new levels of concensus on new aspects of the race question, through the clash of ideas and power involved in creative disorder, then

---

[4] Such a new and specialized federal police force might become especially necessary if major changes in international relations—such as world disarmament—were to cause major reductions or abolition of the large American military establishment, if the suggestion made in Chapter XI is correct —that the creation of this large military force after 1940 helped reduce mass private violence.

new enforceable "law" would presumably be created and the responsibility for dealing with the areas covered by the new laws would shift from agencies behaving like a "state" to agencies behaving like a "government."

The second of what seem to be the crucial prerequisites to avoiding racial violence—the invention and legitimation of new forms of controlled creative disorder that would be applicable to new areas of racial conflict—may have some implications and effects that go beyond the racial arena. As in the extension of the legitimacy of the free press beyond the issues and social groups for which it was first espoused to new issues and other social groups, so it is possible that some forms of creative disorder invented by Negroes in the movement for racial equality will become legitimate for other social groups as well. For example, it is not impossible to imagine some of the white miners of eastern Kentucky, many of whom have been without jobs for many years, sitting-in on federal unemployment compensation offices. It is not impossible to imagine school boycotts by students protesting the firing of a professor, or protesting against their schools being put on a split-shift schedule. In other words, if the new forms of disorder become legitimate there is no reason to expect that only Negroes will find them useful and necessary.[5]

The new techniques are also likely to revivify the practice of that kind of democracy in which all the citizens participate directly, in which each man has an active share in the shaping of his own destiny and that of his society. For it is in the nature of the new forms of disorder that they are creative in two ways. Not only do they help to reshape the society, they reshape those who carry on the disorder. It takes a much deeper commitment on the part of much larger numbers of people to carry on a school boycott or a rent strike or a mass public march than it does to pursue a more orderly politics. The new forms of disorder involve large numbers of people in the process of politics, they make that process immediate and relevant and productive for people who before were outside of politics and fearful or destructive of it. In this sense those who carried the signs that

---

[5] These words were written before, and seem to be partially confirmed by, the use of sit-ins by students in the Free Speech Movement at the University of California in December 1964.

called for "Freedom Now" during the racial conflict of the early 1960s may have been more accurate than many of them knew. They were thinking about racial "freedom," which they soon discovered would take time to achieve and would come only "tomorrow," not "now." But to the extent that the very act of protest and the creation of new sorts of politics activated those who had been politically apathetic, it freed men who had been unfree. Thus the very process of creating disorder in the hope of racial "freedom tomorrow" was helpful in bringing individual "Freedom Now." Just as the disorderly pamphleteering press focused the energies of the urban middle class and the disorderly labor movement focused the energies of working men, so the new forms of disorder have already indicated they have the power to create a politically alive citizenry out of the Negro Americans who have been one of the last of America's excluded groups.

Chapter Three

Forms of Action: Normal Politics

As we have seen, Arthur Waskow finds the most creative aspect of the New Left to be its experimentation with new forms of political expression.

Yet, during the last decade, the Left has also tried following the traditional paths of coalition and electoral politics. The hope was that electoral politics, indeed elected officials, might give legitimacy to the campaign against poverty, racism and the war. Such hope, and the activity that followed, was at its height in 1966—with the Congressional Peace candidates, and during 1968. The McCarthy campaign created a coalition of young liberals and radicals. For an historical moment it appeared as if an electoral revolution was possible in America. The loss of McCarthy, as well as the defeat suffered by most of the peace candidates in 1966, left behind a legacy of bitterness and alienation.

But from a New Left point of view, neither electoral success nor failure are crucial matters. In the section that follows, although noting the real challenge that the peace candidates posed for their opponents, Andrew Kopkind, too, documents the tensions that arose between running of a successful campaign and the creation and care of a radical movement. The issue was this: should the radicalism of the movement be sacrificed so as to create a broader appeal to the electorate.

In his letter to the supporters of Senator McCarthy, Carl Oglesby answers that question in the negative. Oglesby admits that the campaign is important in the sense that it marks a split in the Democratic coalition. In addition, he demands as well a complementary vision by New Left activists. The McCarthy candidacy brought the issue of the war into the political arena, but, according to Oglesby, McCarthy-esque politics will not transform the system that made the war. Building a radical movement, in his view, is the first priority of the New Left.

Anti-Vietnam Politics*
Peace Candidates in Oregon, California

Andrew Kopkind

At last count, there were 103 candidates running on the "peace issue" for public office this year. The count is going down. Among the dead or wounded in last week's round of primaries was Howard Morgan, whose rather frail campaign for the Democratic senatorial nomination in Oregon had been elevated to a kind of national referendum on Vietnam. Oregon turned out to be ill-suited to the test. Its politicians are accustomed to playing to a small house; no one knew quite what to make of the network television crews, the national political reporters and columnists, and the obvious concern of the Johnson Administration. In the end, only a minority of voters cast what was essentially a protest vote on a single issue. Duncan's majority was over 70,000.

Morgan's campaign was hardly a departure from political convention. He admitted that on most issues he had "very few differences" with his opponent, Rep. Robert Duncan, whom he had urged to run in the first place. Morgan got into the race

---

* Reprinted with permission from The New Republic, June 4, 1966.

himself when Duncan declared that he "would rather fight Communism on the Mekong than on the Columbia," and was supporting the Administration's Vietnam policy. Senator Wayne Morse rushed to Morgan's side, and the two set out around the state to "talk sense" about the war. Morgan tried to explain that "the catchword and slogan—'Communism' "—was the ruination of US foreign policy, but it was never clear that he was not caught by the same word. He often put his opposition to the war in anti-Communist terms: "When Communism is stopped in the backward nations it will be stopped by offering a better life to the people," he said in a televised debate with Duncan. It sounded like an ad for the Agency for International Development.

In the precinct headquarters around the state, Morgan's campaign workers were trying to keep it respectable. In Eugene, Oregon's second largest city and the home of the state university, they excluded campus activists from the campaign ("the beards made people nervous," one worker said). And despite the national publicity, the campaign centered more and more on Morgan's personality, on images, and old political alliances. That was Morgan's downfall. He is intelligent and tough, and he had a good record in the Democratic Party (as state chairman, he helped bring the Democrats to power in the 1950s) and as a strongly pro-public power state utilities commissioner, and later Federal Power Commissioner. But he spoke poorly, on television, he was stiff in contrast to Duncan's crew-cut, slightly rumpled, snoose-chewing ease. Unable to find a new base of voters, or even to form a new electoral coalition, Morgan had to fish for votes from the same pool as Duncan, and by the normal political standards he made an inferior match. No one in Oregon was particularly happy with the war; but it took an act of will, such as voters in statewide elections rarely exercise, to single out the issue and supply it to a candidate who was not very exciting in any other way. "Everybody who votes for Morgan is against the war," a Democrat said shortly before the primary, "but not everybody who votes for Duncan is for it."

The Morgan campaign is likely to be a model for most of the other peace candidates around the country, in the primaries and on election day in November. Few will fare much better. In California, there are 30 such announced candidates, for offices from attorney general down to assemblyman. A few incumbents will probably be reelected on their overall records, but not many of the insurgents can break through on an anti-Vietnam platform alone. Even in California, where the frantic volunteer organizations give issues a prominence they have nowhere else, the war is not going to redraw the political map this year. The polls are probably right: all else equal, the active anti-war vote is a stable minority. There is one startling exception.

The campaign to take the Democratic congressional nomination from Rep. Jeffrey Cohelan in California's 7th District (Berkeley and part of Oakland) is the most ambitious, and possibly the most successful attempt so far to reshape policy to deal with the deep conflicts in American society that the "consensus" glosses over: poverty, powerlessness, war. The campaign began without a candidate. Last year, a Berkeley physician wrote to Cohelan asking for a strong statement against the war; Cohelan (in his own terms a "liberal intellectual" and "more dove than hawk") replied that he supported the Administration's position. The physician wrote again, and when Cohelan once more demurred, he began to think seriously about organizing a primary fight against the congressman.

At the same time, the militant anti-war protest on the University of California campus was playing itself out. The Vietnam Day Committee had replaced the Free Speech Movement as the expression of student radicalism. In October, the VDC brought 15,000 people into the streets of Berkeley. But the war did not end, and the marches began to get smaller. Many of the students came to believe that the shock effect of direct action was not enough, that it was necessary to exert pressure directly on the men running or condoning the war at the polls.

The physician, and a group of like-minded professionals and businessmen who had come together because of their opposition to the war, had precisely the same idea. And it was not long before the two rather disparate elements in Berkeley met and produced a candidate, Robert Scheer, to oppose Cohelan.

Scheer had been the intellectual star, although not the political leader, of the VDC. He was, off and on, a graduate student in Asia affairs, had visited Vietnam, and had spoken and written on the war (for *Ramparts* magazine, where he

is an editor, and in a long report to the Center for the Study
of Democratic Institutions). He had been around the Berkeley
campus for almost six years, and at 30 was able to travel
between the worlds of student activism and grown-up left-
wing politics. He had a neatly trimmed beard and a Brooks
Brothers suit.

A Multi-Issue Movement

The Scheer-for-Congress campaign began last winter more
as a brainstorm than as a carefully planned professional effort.
Offices were set up in various parts of the district, and volun-
teers wandered through looking for odd chores and precinct
assignments. It was unclear to most of them what it all meant
as a protest against the war. During the winter, the VDC
staged a sit-in at Cohelan's office in downtown Oakland; Scheer
led it. Grown-ups in the Berkeley hills began to worry. Then
in March, Scheer officially filed as a candidate in the June 7
Democratic primary, and the student radicals were seized
with anxiety: the purity of the movement was tainted by its
acceptance of the Democratic Party label.

It may have pained some of the students to work at
registering Democratic voters, but by the end of the registration drive, there were 10,000 new names on the rolls. In
Berkeley, the increase was nearly five times the statewide
average for the period. More headquarters were opened, campaign committees began to expand operations, and slowly a
sense of excitement spread. The "hill people" — the older
liberals — who'se enthusiasm had waned as the campaign
seemed to become more radical, came back to support Scheer
when they saw its mounting popularity. Many of the students
who had dropped out when the campaign seemed to lose its
ideological purity ("electoral politics is a drag," one of them
said), returned.

What had happened was that the campaign had become
a multi-issue movement, concerned not only with the war, but
with the plight of Oakland's notorious ghettos, with the failure
of the poverty program, with school segregation, civil liberties,
urban renewal, job discrimination, police brutality — the
whole range of issues which the traditional political leaders

in the community either denied or ignored. Scheer tried to tie them all together as functions of the powerlessness of ordinary people. To change their condition, people had to use power — to challenge leaders as well as support them.

No one had challenged Jeffrey Cohelan in a long time. He is, in Scheer's words, "a perfect spokesman for the liberal consensus." His voting record is near-perfect on the ADA index, and he is the devil incarnate to the right wing. Cohelan is 52; he grew up in poverty in San Francisco, went to the University of California, drove a milk-truck for a time, and became a business agent for the Teamsters Union. He had a Fulbright research fellowship to Oxford and Leeds. He was elected to Congress in 1958 in the statewide Democratic sweep behind Pat Brown's devastation of William Knowland (in the "right-to-work" fight).

Cohelan epitomizes the political style against which the Scheer campaign has set itself in diametrical opposition. Cohelan stays in Washington, works on "the inside," deals with leaders, and keeps his doubts about his party and its policies to himself. He treats the House of Representatives with unashamed respect and wants above all to be "a good working member." "You've got to make your way with your peers," he told me recently on one of his infrequent visits to his district. He speaks of his "two constituencies" — the voters at home, and his fellows in the House. He does not wish to get too involved in foreign affairs, for "the House isn't a forum for foreign policy debates. There is all that busy-busy-ness—no time for homework." Nevertheless, he has given 18 speeches in the House on Vietnam. (Sample: "Learned observers disagree as to just how this war developed, and historians of the future will debate the wisdom of specific policy decisions of the past 12 years. The one thing on which all reasonable men can agree is that we want to end this war, with its terrible toll of lives and its tremendous drain on the resources of this and other countries, as soon as possible.") Like Vice President Humphrey, Cohelan believes the most effective way to end the war is to provide "counter-pressure to the hawks on the other side of the President," preferably in a low tone of voice.

For Cohelan, the hard work of protest is over. "I was an organizer for a labor union. I was on the barricades — re-

forming everything," he said nostalgically on a foggy afternoon in his Oakland office. "Now we're trying to solve the
problem in governmental ways. The basic legislative work is
done, although there is unquestionably a mopping-up operation
left to do."

The Congressman's Real Job

For Scheer, reform has hardly begun. "If we are serious about
making the political process relevant to people's lives," he
said, "it is not enough to formulate a program. Social change
will not come as a gift from those presently in power. They
know that people must fight for what they believe in." Scheer
sees the House as a forum and very little else. The real job
of the congressman, Scheer thinks, is in his constituency, educating and organizing voters — not only to elect the candidate,
but to bring pressure along a line of issues. His campaign
has hooked up with groups in the district protesting discrimination, school segregation, the administration of the poverty
program, the police, and, of course, Vietnam. Electoral politics—and an elected official—in effect could provide the "cover"
for direct action, much in the way that labor's candidates have
given a kind of protection to union activism.

The Scheer workers are supposed to be organizers, not
salesmen. They are blunt with the voters, and bring up issues
as sharply as they can. They encourage argument, and strangely
enough, the process seems to be working. Precinct workers
are not thrown out of living rooms. They find support where
they least expect it, among people who like to be treated honestly
and think they have never been before (Scheer makes a point
of attacking politicians in general, as well as in particular).

The confrontation of liberal and radical styles is perhaps
uniquely possible in the 7th District at this point. "We're
cheating in a way," Scheer said, for there is a congruence of
factors which has made his campaign possible. For 10 years
a loose community of radicals has been growing in the San
Francisco Bay area. It antedates both the student protest and
the civil rights movement of the early sixties. Starting with
the remnants of the old base carved out by Jack London, then
by Harry Bridges and the Longshoremen's Union, the newer

radicals began their careers demonstrating against the Un-American Activities Committee, then the Caryl Chessman protest and the formation of a student political organization called SLATE at Berkeley in 1957; the civil rights sit-ins in San Francisco followed, then the Free Speech Movement, and the VDC. A variety of radical activities are now considered legitimate—even tame—in San Francisco that would provoke tear gas and mass arrests in other cities. The Scheer campaign finds support all over the San Francisco area, not just in the 7th Congressional District.

The juxtaposition of the most politically active university population in the country and a large, unorganized, predictably explosive ghetto creates an opening for "movement" politics. The eagerness of the more or less affluent (and more or less intellectual) "hill people" to give money and support, and the enthusiasm of a corps of precinct workers toughened by years of volunteer work in the liberal California Democratic Council clubs were added ingredients in the campaign.

But over the months the Scheer campaign has developed its own singular dynamic. It has attracted a strange collection of types: scientists (biologist and mathematicians) from the University who had never worked before in politics, liberals from the hills unaccustomed to the sight of a beard, students from beat to frat, ghetto Negroes, housewives. There are said to be three or four "card-carrying" Communists actively in the campaign (they are of the young, DuBois Club variety), and they are considered in the "conservative wing" ("they never want to rock the boat, they always want to make deals," a campaign worker complained). No one is excluded from the campaign if he agrees with the "draft platform" and the general approach, but within those limits there are tensions. Until the last weeks before the June 7 primary, campaign decisions were made in free-for-all strategy sessions open to all workers. They lasted for hours; the strategists argued bitterly over the wording of bumper stickers (the left-wing position was that the slogan should be bigger than the name of the candidate; the right wing won that fight), posters and ads. The ambience was something between a college seminar and a SNCC conference, but in some mysterious way decisions evolved. In the last hectic days, a 12-man strategy committee was empowered to set policy, but the old style hardly changed.

Toward the end, the campaign had a thousand workers ringing doorbells in the district. Original estimates of a 25-percent (at most) protest vote were raised. Two weeks before the primary, Cohelan's advisers hoped they could keep the Scheer vote down to 40 percent. Cohelan has the AFL-CIO endorsement (the Political Education Committee never let Scheer come to speak before it), but Scheer has the Long-shoremen (with 6,000 families in the district) as well as other independent unions. Scheer was endorsed by the district's California Democratic Council convention, which was filled with anti-war members; it was the first time the CDC has refused to endorse a Democratic incumbent congressman.

"A Man Whose Career Is the House"

Cohelan is worried and bitter. He got Postmaster General Larry O'Brien to come to the district for a campaign testimonial dinner (Cohelan is on the House Appropriations subcommittee on the Post Office), and he procured telegrams of endorsement from senators and representatives. But he sees his consti-tuency falling apart. "I'm really on the rack now," he said, with three weeks to go in the campaign. "I'm going to win this election, but I'll have to give my bloody soul to do it. The people who worry me are the people who say, 'You're the greatest guy in the world, but I want to get at Johnson.' Scheer's campaign doesn't mean anything except that a lot of people in this district don't like President Johnson. People are warm and friendly here, but when they get around to Johnson they begin to snarl. It's small satisfaction that it's not directed to me. I have a great compassion for the process that's going on— the 'New Left' and the student protests. But now I find myself a victim of it. It's kind of a Greek tragedy, and I have to play out my role."

A Democratic colleague recently characterized Cohelan as "a man whose whole career is the House." He has no law practice or real estate firm or family business to fall back on. He likes "making it" in the House. He has an inside track already in the Appropriations Committee, and his friends in

Congress suspect that he may have an eye on a position in the Democratic leadership. In a way, the primary campaign is already a failure for Cohelan, for in the world of images and popularity he has suffered some telling blows. "It's not just a war protest vote any more," a labor official in Cohelan's campaign remarked ruefully when only 25 people turned up for the big AFL-CIO "mobilization" to do precinct work in the district. Labor, the Negroes who follow the old leaders allied with Cohelan, and the large numbers of people who are not at all prepared to "risk" a radical congressman ("I don't think the Republic will fall if I'm elected," Scheer says) will probably return Cohelan, and he will not have much trouble against the right-wing Republican candidate in November. But his "peers" in the House might think a little less of his power when he goes back to Washington next January.

The Scheer campaign has a predicament of its own. If it loses, the campaigners must decide how and whether their movement can be maintained. Scheer has said that he will stay in the district, and he may run as a write-in candidate in November. But there may be better ways than electoral campaigns to gain recognition for the unrecognized in Oakland. Increasingly as the campaign progressed, it began to be directed more toward energizing the Oakland ghetto than condemning "Johnson's war." There are many in the campaign who think that the ghetto is the logical place to start in a campaign to change foreign policy.

After the primary next week, the tensions between the CDC liberals and the VDC radicals are going to show up in greater relief. The old conflict between "freedom" and "movement" is present already; here the fight is between the "Scheer" and the "campaign" elements—those who will take short cuts (make deals with other politicians, push the personality of the candidate instead of the issues, soften positions on issues) to win more votes against those who want to keep a radical movement going.

If the campaign is less than pure, it is still a departure from politics as usual. Some of the older politicians can hardly believe what they see. "Scheer really thinks that people vote on issues," Cohelan's campaign manager said one day recently. He couldn't understand it. "People don't vote for issues. They vote for a man—to represent them in Congress. Well," he said, "if Scheer is right, we're out."

Governor's parties, headed and directed by whatever man who calls himself a Democrat happens to be in power at the time.

The Southern task, therefore, is building a party of some kind, calling it either "Democrat" or "Freedom Democrats" or whatever.

In Georgia, a first step toward that goal has been taken. There is a state-wide organization here called the Democratic Forum. It was this group that called the convention that elected the challenge delegation that went to the Chicago Convention.

My hope is that this group can become a party, or more correctly, an organized group of Georgians who place high priority on electoral politics a great deal to the left of the organized electoral politics so common to this region.

That process, if it is to be successful, will take nearly eight or ten years, I believe, and a lot of hard work and a lot of money.

Black people in Georgia are a state-wide minority, although we are a majority in some counties and will be a majority in Atlanta within five years. In these areas I would favor all-black (or at worst, majority black) political organizations that could effectively, democratically, direct the political thrust of a group of people for whom politics means both street improvements and civilizing the police, as well as a chance to influence and direct policy-making on a city, county and state level.

For this election, in November, what strikes me as the biggest difference between Southern and Northern outlooks is that most Kennedy-McCarthy supporters I know in this region are hoping for, if not working for, the election of Vice-President Humphrey because of their fear of the Strom Thurmond influence in a Nixon government, while their Northern counterparts are mostly not participating in the November election on a presidential level.

Those of us here, of course, are subjected to much abuse by those persons unfortunate enough not to have to live here. We are called "shills" and "prostitutes" by our Northern brothers and sisters, which is an indication, I believe, that now that the sit-in demonstrations and Freedom Rides have paled, and voter registration efforts lost their excitement, that there isn't much interest up yonder in us folks down here. But that's life.

An Open Letter to McCarthy Supporters

by Carl Oglesby

Is McCarthy the pay-off of those years of protest? Does he represent the partial fruition of our efforts to build a movement for changing America?

Or is he only another attempt to emasculate that protest? Is he what the Movement has been working for? Or against?

How in fact are we to define McCarthy so that we can at least be sure that we're talking about the same thing?

Perhaps by his record? Surely you're tired by now of listening to the dreary list of his illiberal votes: his assent to the witch-hunt politics of the '50s (as late as 1959 he voted for the Student Loyalty Oath Bill), his vacillation on civil rights (in 1961 he voted against witholding Federal aid from segregated schools), his occasional anti-Labor stands (against extension of minimum-wage coverage in 1960 and against the rail workers in 1963), and maybe most galling of all, the tardiness of his opposition to the War (he voted for every war appropriation bill, for the Tonkin Gulf resolution, and against the 1966 amendment which would have exempted non-volunteering draftees from service in Vietnam). He has consistently opposed the admission of China to the UN, and clings to the view that there is nothing structurally wrong with our foreign policy: "We still have the fleet," he said last November, "we still have Japan, we still have a position in South Korea, we have built up a strong base in Thailand . . . " And in April, asked if we needed to take a new approach to international affairs, he answered "No. We do in Vietnam, in Southeast Asia. But not in Korea, not in Japan, not in India, not the North Atlantic Treaty Organization."

But you have heard this.

You are doubtless a little worried about the suggestion of hypocrisy in his dissent. He sought to provide an alternative, he said when he announced his candidacy last November, to those who "become cynical and make threats of support for third parties or fourth parties or other irregular political movements." As if so explicit a subordination of content to form were anything but the essence of cynicism.

You have often been informed, moreover, that his chances of victory are galactically remote. You knew this, after all, from the start.

So add it up.

His record: to be charitable, call it ambiguous.

His present policies: to give the benefit of the doubt, say that they do not quite hit the nail on the head.

His real power: to be optimistic, assume that it is still in the process of formation

What is the sum?

McCarthy-in-Practice

A definition of McCarthy-in-practice: the probably unproductive compromise of policies which are ambiguous, if not dubious, to begin with.

Which is merely one way of putting what most of you already claim to know.

Then why do you continue to support him?

We think there are reasons. One has to do with an illusion. Another with a reality. And another with a failure of nerve.

You visualize McCarthy as a man in the process of change. You imply that he should no more be judged by what he used to be than, for example, SDS itself.

In a time like this, that is no ground for fantasy. Above all we need clarity now, not subtle evocations of mood. And in the measure that McCarthy has been clear, his case against the War remains explicitly a traditional case for anti-Communist containment.

It was only his dedication to the containment policy which led him to challenge the Administration in the first place. He saw the truth to which political vanity had blinded Johnson,

namely that it was not possible to impose upon the Vietnamese
a government of French colonial officers, and that the desperate
attempt to do so was creating the gravest crisis of the Cold
War period: it was cracking the Atlantic Alliance. Not alone
in his awareness, he was also not the first to voice it. We do
not say that his decision to oppose Johnson openly was easy.
Within its own framework, it was perhaps even courageous.
But this courage is that of the timid among the craven, the
diffident among the abject, the whisperer among the silent.
There are other standards of courage in a world which remem-
bers Ché Guevara, meets again every day the ordinary Vietnam
peasant, and knows Fanny Lou Hamer. Compared to what
we need, in any case, his distinction is a small excursion from
an abysmal norm.

We think you project onto the future McCarthy the virtues
which you know he must come to posses. The current moral
and physical turmoil certainly seems to beg for heroes.
McCarthy is honest. He has candor and integrity and intelligence enough to distinguish victory from defeat. With a desperation which we can easily understand, you treat him as
if he were already the man he has not yet even promised to
become. This is illusionment.

The Reality: It is just that Left politics in America is
hard. There is not much room for movement in that direction.
Not much is possible. Play to secure the marginal victory and
avoid the central defeat.

So it comes down to the famous bird in hand.

If it does nothing else, the McCarthy campaign represents
itself implicitly as the Leftmost ideological position at which
political realism still endures. Above all, you have told us,
this is no time for utopia, romance, or extremist provocations.
The very power of the case the New Left made for stopping
the War, in fact, is a conclusive argument for an expedient
politics. So McCarthy won't join the Vietcong. At least he'll
bring off the capitulation without totally freaking everybody out.

Don't demand the final salvation of the whole world
tomorrow.

Demand, instead, the end of the War today.

Don't demand socialism tomorrow.

Demand, instead, that capitalism, starting today, begin creating for itself a more human heart.

Don't demand for tomorrow that real democracy establish itself in our society.

Demand, instead, that the old elites at once start behaving better.

Very tempting, this realism of ideals, and we ourselves will cheerfully confess a preference for effectiveness over usefulness.

But this practicality—with respect to exactly what policies does it commend itself to us? How desirable in themselves are these policies? And how exclusively are they the property of McCarthy?

McCarthy has already persuaded us that his overriding objective is the defense of the same American Empire which we find flatly unsupportable. That he should see the cessation of large-scale military action against Vietnam as the precondition of revamped containment/imperialism—we find this not at all hard to understand. This is also why the big corporations have turned against the War. They, too, want to find new security for those key positions in Europe and Latin America which the Vietnam "diversion" has left exposed. They, too, are passionately concerned about the international equilibrium of the dollar, and they understand that a sharp de-esclation of the War is a basic current requirement for the health of the North Atlantic economic system.

McCarthy (and Rockefeller), among all the candidates, possibly understood this best, maybe even first. That may be commendable. The point, however, is that in one way or another the futility of the War has become clear even to Nixon. Any President must contrive to abandon the War. The Vietnamese have so decreed.

McCarthy's campaign is important. It is one manifestation of the breakdown of the political coalitions put together in the 1930s. At least indirectly, it expresses the emergence of a newly politicized and activist "grass roots" constituency— that of the post-war generations. It imperfectly embodies the new spirit of participant democracy.

But practicality? Realism? Granted the sincerity of his

occasional New Left-sounding flourishes, McCarthy's "practicality" amounts in the end to the adulteration of the necessary critique of the War, the obscuring of its sources in the system of American expansionism. It amounts to a moderating of already timid proposals which therefore lose whatever character they might have had: better negotiations, maybe, inviting the NLF into a coalition whose other elements are precisely the forces which the NLF has been struggling to expel and which have precious-little constituency other than the US State Department, and on all other problems of foreign policy the retention and even reinforcing of the Truman-to-Johnson containment line.

No question: Such a policy is "practical," "possible," and "realistic." We've had it for years.

And we haven't even raised yet the most obvious question: Since so many of you argue that we New Leftists should have compromised a bit for the sake of this "realistic alternative" we wonder why so few of you have argued that McCarthy can win?

The Failure of Nerve: Almost every young supporter of McCarthy we talk with is well to the Left of his champion. Many express the same dissatisfactions with his policies that we have expressed. Almost nobody thinks there is more than a hundred-to-one chance of his winning. The bird in the hand which was supposed to justify all sorts of tactical compromises turns out on inspection to be only a possible bird in the hand.

Then why all the excitement about "really making a difference"?

We have to say this bluntly:

We think you are afraid of your own politics, and that you are employing the McCarthy campaign as a means of making your dissent look respectable and "legitimate."

Fear of honest thought and its political imperatives; of effecting a clean break with the powerful institutions which have squandered so many lives; of abandoning the security of the system whose outrages you attack; of becoming your own "base of legitimacy": Is McCarthy a reprieve?

So What Do We Want You To Do?

Above all, to understand your own importance.

Not to borrow others' causes for fear of the difficulty of your own.

To grasp the fact that the authenticity which you find in McCarthy is there only because you have put it there; that his special virtues are merely small versions of your common possibilities.

Honesty? Yes. You are more honest.

Rebelliousness? Yes. Your rebellion is better, even if it has not yet discovered its proper gait and idiom. You dance better. You write better poems.

The only really interesting practicality of his campaign, in fact, is that it has your support. He needs you. The institutions which have mis-educated, mis-employed, mis-ruled your lives need you.

You don't need them.

This battle, after all, is one that we have begun: the young ones began it, not the old ones. Only the young ones will be loyal to it. The old ones remember too many defeats and erroneous victories. It is our generation's fight. For obvious reasons, its imagery condenses around Vietnam, America's ghettos, the inflicted poverty of the Third World. But its underlying content goes beyond them.

We think that the present stakes are immense. What we think is happening, in all this confusing and frightening disorder, is the unfolding of a new stage of human history, the writing by a new generation of a new human agenda—old in its essential hopes, new in the possibility of their realization.

A birth is trying to take place. Certain high-class killers in league with certain clowns are trying to hold the baby back, while a few political priests suggest politely that the birth of a little finger might be permissible. In behalf of everything old, used up, and dying—in other words, in behalf of their own privilege—they fight against everything new. So many undertakers in the delivery room.

The point is not to make deals with them there, but to get them out.

"That cannot happen."

Perhaps that is true. But since it must happen, it will, and whether it can or not makes no difference.

Like most of us, you are mostly of the middle and upper-middle classes. We have not been hungry, cold, or afraid. We have grown up with the Cold War, which made anxiety an ordinary state, and the Machine, a presence in our lives at once abstract and immediate, and which made habit of miracle.

Our task is first to clarify the main issues of the world we must live in.

Revolutionary communism? That is the primary form taken on by the struggles of the forcibly dispossessed to re-possess themselves of the identity and destiny. American power has no business opposing those struggles. Americans indeed must learn to rejoice in the human bravery that brings them into being. For when those who are now oppressed are not oppressed, then the masters will also be liberated from their permanently desperate vigils.

The militant nationalism of American blacks? Far from being a threat to us, this anger enriches us and we welcome it. There is no man, no law, no government that can substitute for this creative movement of the people.

The defense of property rights? Americans have already been de-propertied by the very system whose demand for property worship is most feverish. Our task is not to lament this event, but to move forward through it. We do not deny that once upon a time property rights constituted the base of the development of social wealth. Men paid a high price in suffering for the political guarantee of these rights to a privileged elite. There is no longer the remotest need for either that suffering, that guarantee, or that elite. Current and future wealth is wholly socialized in every respect but that ownership. The completion of its socialization is the only way to avoid the on-coming international war of race and class and to restore the chance of national sanity.

Our parallel task is to create the political means by which we can pursue our objectives.

This requires, above all, that we face a simple fact: Political institutions designed to perpetuate a system of power will never become instruments for the transformation of that system.

If you want to stop not only the Vietnam War but the

system that begot it, if you want not merely to blur the edges of racism but to change the system that needed slaves in the first place and could "emancipate" them only into ghettos in the second, if you want not merely to make deals with irrationality but to liberate reason for the conquest of joy, then you will have to go outside the system for the preparation of your means. You will have to go inside yourself first to rediscover the feeling of your own possible freedom, and from there to the feeling of the possible freedom of others.

Pride and communion.

That's what the Movement is about. That's what we think you should be about.

Chapter Four

Forms of Action: Extraordinary Politics

A. The Politics of Protest

Sympathetic liberals often define New Left politics as the politics of protest and probe no further. However, as we shall see in the following articles, the danger as it is perceived from the Left is that opposition may be frozen into "mere protest." The New Left seeks to move beyond protest and its dependence upon a response from the Establishment.

Though members of the New Left tend to discredit the notion that protest alone can force effective change, they have often utilized the possibilities inherent in this limited form of action.

In the section that follows, Kenneth Boulding emphasizes those elements that the Left believes proceed from successful protest: politicalization of the public, sometimes accompanied by active involvement in the movement. The teach-ins, Boulding says, are not only an act of opposition toward politics but an effort to build a powerful movement through political education as well.

Marches, demonstrations and moratoriums perform much the same function in Boulding's view. Through them, he states, the participant makes his protest a matter of public record and inter- acts with those who share his sentiments.

The politics of protest are, however, subject to calculations in numerical terms that can subvert their radical thrust. In this section, the comments by the Editors of *Studies on The Left*, a periodical now defunct, as well as Jeremy Brecher's discussion on the October 15th moratorium, illustrate the danger of confining radical politics to protest.

At the end of the decade another form of protest took shape: the political trial. In the conclusion of this section, Rennie Davis discusses the radical potential of this method of protest. In order to properly use the political trial, Davis says, the defendants must reverse roles with the prosecution. The defendants must act to demonstrate the injustices of society and the complicity of the political authorities when the government seeks to establish their guilt. The purpose of this, according to Davis, is to catch the attention of the indifferent and compel them to observe and to listen.

Reflections on Protest*

Kenneth E. Boulding

In a way, the forerunner of (the teach-in) movement was the remarkable mobilization of faculty members on university campuses against Goldwater, which represented political arousal on a scale which has rarely, if ever, been seen before in these supposedly cloistered circles. The teach-in movement is clearly a response to Johnson's behaving like Goldwater and so, in a way, is part of this same arousal.

Nobody, unfortunately, is much concerned to study the effects of all this, some of which may be quite different from what the people who are aroused by the arousal intend. I am constantly impressed by the ironies of the social systems, where action often produces quite the reverse of the consequences

* Reprinted by permission of Science and Public Affairs, the Bulletin of Atomic Scientists. Copyright © 1970 by the Educational Foundation for Nuclear Science.

which are intended. On the other hand, presumably, the better our knowledge of social systems, the more likely are we to avoid any unintentional consequences. It is important, therefore, for protesters to have some theory of protest and to be sensitive to those circumstances in which protest is effective in achieving its intended consequences, and those circumstances in which it is not. . . .

Unlike the civil rights movement which had fulfilled almost all the conditions of successful protest, the peace movement only fulfills some of them. The condition which it fulfills is that related to the long-run payoff. There is no doubt that the payoffs of a stable peace are enormous. The $120 billion a year that the world spends on the war industry is an appalling waste, which may well set back the achievement of world development by even hundreds of years and might even prevent it altogether. The probability of long-run change toward a system of stable peace is therefore high, and the peace movement fulfills this one essential requirement for the success of a movement for social change. On the other hand, it fulfills practically none of the other conditions. Its objectives, in terms of specific institutional and behavioral change, are not clear. We still do not really know how to get stable peace and what particular forms of behavior lead us toward, rather than away from, this goal. There is, furthermore, a great diversity of view as to immediate objectives within the peace movement.

It is clear, also, that American society at least is not supersaturated in regard to social change toward stable peace. In a sense, the task of the peace movement is fundamentally education, rather than protest. Most of the communications which are received by Americans, whether in the formal educational system or in the informal contacts of face to face conversation, tend to create an image of the world in which war is a recurrent necessity and in which, furthermore, for the United States, war has paid off pretty well. We tend to associate war with easy victories, like the war against Mexico or Spain, or with periods of economic prosperity and recovery from depression, as in World War II. We are not, and never have been, a peace-loving nation; we are not only ruthless and bloody but feel no shame about it. There is nothing in our Constitution; in our national heroes, many of whom are generals; in our national origin, which came out of a war; in our greatest single national experience, which was the Civil War; or in anything contributing to our national image that makes war illegitimate in the way racial discrimination is felt to be illegitimate and inconsistent with our national ideals. In the case of war, we have very little hypocrisy, and change is very difficult. The peace movement is not simply trying to mobilize an already existing mass feeling or sentiment; it is trying to create a radical change in the national image, against which all the forces of ordinary legitimacy seem to be arrayed. In the case of the peace movement, therefore, protest arouses counterprotest with great ease. The hawks in our society far outnumber the doves, and those who flutter the dovecotes stand in danger of arousing clouds of hawks from their innumerable nests. It will take an extensive process of education and, perhaps, even the grim teacher of national disaster before we learn that the prevailing national image is incompatible with our wellbeing or even with our survival; we have yet to learn that we are only one people among many, that we are not the rulers of the world, that power cannot be exercised without legitimacy, and that the costs of stable peace, significant and important as they are, are far less than the benefits.

The teach-in movement represents, perhaps, a partly subconscious recognition of the validity of some of the above principles. It began as a movement of pure protest and outrage. The motivations which inspired it were no doubt various. They included a genuine fear of escalation into nuclear warfare; they included also a sense of moral outrage at the use of such things as napalm and the "lazy dog," and the appalling sufferings which we are imposing on the Vietnamese in the supposed name of freedom and democracy. Coupled with this, unquestionably, were some people on the left who were politically sympathetic with the objectives of the Vietcong, though in the original movement there were few if any of these. I am inclined to think that the largest motivating factor was a sense of simple human sympathy with the sufferings of the Vietnamese, a sense of outrage at the utterly inhuman weapons of the American air force, and a sense of outrage, also, that we were using Vietnamese as the guinea pigs in weapon experimentation. The method of protest first suggested by the original group at the University of Michigan was a work moratorium and a one-day suspension of classes.

This violated a good many of the above principles. It is a form of protest which is not related to the object of protest; it immediately aroused a large counterprotest over the means, as well as over the object of protest, and it was very strongly on the protest side of the spectrum and away from education. The teach-in, which was adopted as a substitute, was much more successful. It at least edged toward the education end of the spectrum, even though it still retained a good many of the qualities of protest, and it was appropriate to the situation. The teach-in movement, furthermore, seems to be developing more and more in the direction of dialogue rather than pure protest, and this itself reflects the fact that there is an educational task ahead rather than a task of pure protest. The basic problem here is change in the national image itself, and this is something which protest is singularly unable to do, for protest has to take the image for granted and call attention to certain inconsistencies and incompatibilities. It assumes a given national image and says, in effect, to the policy-maker, "be consistent with it."

Under these circumstances, what is likely to be the best strategy for those of us who are interested in producing social change toward stable peace? The answer seems fairly clear. It should be a strategy of limited protest and extensive education. We should not, I think, abandon protest altogether, for there are many points even now at which, for instance, the conduct of the war in Vietnam violates a widespread national image of the United States as a reasonably decent and compassionate country. Protest, I suspect, should be directed mainly at the air force; it should be directed at the use of specific weapons which certainly fall under the heading of "cruel and unusual punishments," the moral feeling against which is securely enshrined in our Constitution and history. We have paid enough lip service to the United Nations also, to render protests on this score viable. The contrast between the shred of legitimacy which the United Nations gave us in Korea and the total absence of legitimacy in Vietnam is very striking, and protest could well be concentrated on this. We also have, in our national image, a high value on negotiation and a willingness to negotiate, and our present interpretation of negotiation as the abject surrender of the other side can be protested fiercely and effectively. Beyond this, I suspect, protest will be ineffective, with one possible exception. Our deepest trouble in Vietnam arises out of the total failure of our China policy. At this point, it may well be that the country is ripe for change, and that . . . protest will shake the tree. There is real danger lest, in our obsession with Vietnam, we forget the larger issue and we forget that the solution to Vietnam lies in our relationship with Peking.

Beyond this, social change toward stable peace can only come through education and research. The educational task is to convince people that stable peace is possible. Here we need to point to the many examples in which it has already been achieved. In the educational process, unlike the process of protest, we want to tie in, as far as possible, with existing legitimacy, existing images, and familiar history. We need to play up how we got a security community with the British and the Canadians. We need to play up historical examples of peaceful coexistence, such as was achieved between Protestants and Catholics in the Treaty of Westphalia in 1648. We need to emphasize the continuing dynamic that goes on in socialist countries as well as our own, and to emphasize the learning process and our role as a teacher. We need to emphasize, also, the possible role of the United States not as a great power or as a world dominator but as a leader in the world movement for stable peace. All these things can easily be fitted into existing images and existing legitimacies. Then, at some point, a protest movement may be necessary to crystallize the image as a peace-leader. This may be some time off, but we should be ready for it when it comes.

The Student's March on Washington*

The attempt to make the Mississippi Freedom Democratic Party compromise its demand for recognition at the Democratic National Convention last August, and the attempts to discredit the March on Washington to End the War in Vietnam organized by Students for a Democratic Society this past April, separated out those primarily committed to coalition politics,

---

* Reprinted from *Studies on The Left*, a periodical now defunct.

realignment, or the ideological assumptions of the cold war, from the radical community.

Everyone who sympathized with the MFDP expected that the Johnson forces and all those Democrats anxious to create the enduring image of a competent, united, unruffled party would view the MFDP's demands as disruptive, and would create enormous pressure for submission and compromise. Those who understood something of how the MFDP had been organized, and who the delegates were who gathered outside the Convention Hall in their denim overalls and black dresses, realized that the MFDP would not knuckle under like a temporarily upstart reform club. What was not expected, *except by a very few radicals, was the continuing parade of notables the Johnson forces produced to urge compromise.*

How these people were dragooned into making their appearances and pleas is not important; perhaps Humphrey's nomination seemed conditional, at many points, and dependent on the MFDP's compromise. What is more important is that each of the individuals who urged compromise on the MFDP demonstrated that their loyalty to the Democratic Party, and their assessment that an overwhelming Democratic victory at the polls, was vital for the social changes they favored, outweighed their evaluation of the MFDP's legitimate claims. To urge compromise at Atlantic City was to say, in effect, that it is more important for you in Mississippi, and for all the disadvantaged, that the appearance of unity be preserved, so that the Democratic Party can sweep the elections, then that you should force a party split for a principle which is justified but which can bring you in Mississippi, and all the disadvantaged, no real economic or social amelioration. All the individuals who urged compromise chose the Democratic Party as their agency for social change.

Such is American politics; the Democratic Party, however racist in the past (and present), still retains the legacies of the New Deal and attracts the loyalties of countless individuals who want significant social change and feel that through coalition and realignment the Democratic Party can be transformed into an agency resembling European social democratic parties. So when the small, supposedly undisciplined, grass roots gaggle of Negro sharecroppers, housewives, teachers, ministers and SNCC staff appeared at Atlantic City to demand a recognition which might split the national party, their plea was denied. Individuals once considered radical upbraided the members of the most encouraging local political movement in America, told them to wipe their noses, behave themselves and stop embarrassing the party. Atlantic City demonstrated that there is no room within the Democratic Party for insurgent local groups unwilling to compromise their constituents' demands for national party imperatives.

SDS's March on Washington experienced pressures analogous to those faced by the MFDP. Commitment to coalition politics was a minor cause the pressures brought against the March; of major importance was the animus expressed by many peace leaders against the March's attack on American foreign policy. The following pages are a record of the various attempts by some leaders of the traditional peace movement to control, transform, discredit or sabotage the SDS March.

At its National Council meeting in late December, 1964, Students for a Democratic Society decided to organize a march on Washington to oppose American foreign policy in Vietnam. The event was to be a protest against continuation of the war, but no specific programs or proposals were endorsed or suggested; consensus existed within SDS about the need to protest American involvement; no consensus existed about what steps this country ought to take to disengage.

The National Council also decided that the March would not practice exclusion. SDS would be the sole organizational sponsor, but any group was welcome to join. The decision was taken after a debate which raised all the familiar issues: "undesirable" groups, the possibility of red-baiting, and the fear that key groups would not participate if others were accepted. The National Council (at that December meeting, a forum in which several hundred students participated) decided that they would not exclude groups, that any attempt to formulate standards for participation in the March would result in some form of McCarthyism; the purpose of the March was to provide a focus for the rising student protest against America's involvement in Vietnam; any organization which shared this opposition had to be regarded as legitimate.

Once this was hammered out, the National Council had two choices: it could invite any and every group to co-sponsor the March, or act as the sole sponsor and invite any and every group to participate. For a variety of reasons, the National Council took the second choice. During the first week of January, letters went out to all student political organizations and all the adult peace groups, announcing SDS's plans to hold a March on Washington on April 17, asking endorsement, participation and inviting each group to appoint a liaison.

The left-wing student socialist organizations (DuBois Clubs, Young Socialist Alliance) immediately endorsed the March and promised active participation; the May 2 Movement did not officially endorse the March for several weeks, but indicated its approval. The major peace organizations (SANE, Student Peace Union, Women's International League for Peace and Freedom, Turn Toward Peace, Committee for Non-Violent Action, War Resister's League, Fellowship of Reconciliation) ignored SDS's announcement and invitation. A. J. Muste requested a meeting with SDS staff to discuss the timing of the projected March; April 17 was Easter Sunday, a traditional date for peace group activity. Dave McReynolds of the War Resisters' League wrote to ask whether organizations like the DuBois Clubs would be included. To meet with both men, the SDS staff went to 5 Beekman Street (the offices of *Liberation* magazine Student Peace Union, WRL, FOR New York City headquarters). McReynolds was unhappy about the organization of the March and SDS's failure to take in other groups as equal sponsors; neither he nor Muste offered to formally endorse it.

The SDS National Office received similar objections in the late weeks of January; letters warned that the membership of the several peace organizations would not participate in a demonstration whose sponsorship was solely on the student level and that only several hundred SDS members and die-hard left-wingers would mar the view across Pennsylvania Avenue to the White House. To deal with these objections and consult about the necessary organization, the SDS staff requested a meeting with Bayard Rustin, who had organized three marches on Washington including the August, 1963 March for Jobs and Freedom that brought over 200,000 people to the Capitol. The staff met Rustin at the office of the League for Industrial Democracy (the parent group of SDS), with Michael Harrington (chairman of the Board of the LID) and Tom Kahn (Executive Secretary of the LID) present.

Rustin had several objections to the organization of the march; he was concerned about the style, tone and the groups involved. Most important for Rustin was SDS's failure to present a positive program; he felt that protest without an alternative policy was inadequate and politically irresponsible and that a protest about American involvement had to be clear about the necessity for self-determination in Vietnam. Though Rustin stated that he understood the problems young people have which influenced the style of the SDS march, he felt he could neither endorse nor be part of the March. Rustin pledged technical assistance, and promised not to run down the March or work against it.

The SDS staff agreed that Rustin's position was both legitimate and relevant, and decided to ask him to be one of the speakers. At a second meeting with the same participants, Rustin was invited to speak, but he postponed an immediate decision after some discussion with Harrington and Kahn. Although the SDS staff continually tried to find out whether Rustin had made a decision, they got no answer from him in the following weeks, and finally decided that his refusal to make contact was a refusal to speak. That second meeting was the last time the SDS staff was to have direct contact with Rustin about the March.

As SDS continued its publicity and organization, the Johnson Administration escalated the war; Johnson announced the first official bombing raid of North Vietnamese territory on February 11. On scores of American campuses, the March began to offer means of national protest. Original estimates of the futility and impotence of such a protest were gradually revised; the numbers game began as predicted figures of student marchers climbed week by week. Early in March, Ralph DiGia, Executive Secretary of the War Resisters' League and Bob Karen from the Student Peace Union met with the SDS staff to review the plans for the March. DiGia then set up a meeting of all the traditional peace organizations and asked SDS staff to outline its plans. After the representatives of almost all the peace organizations (SANE, WSP, WILPF, CNVA, WRL, FOR, SPU) considered the plans, they decided that the SDS project should become the national focus of spring activity against the war in Vietnam, that the basic student character of the March should be maintained and other peace organizations should cancel or shift their scheduled activities in deference to it. (SANE had scheduled a "Walk with Dr. Spock" in New York City for April 17, but was persuaded, primarily through pressure from Women's Strike for Peace, to shift its walk to Saturday, April 10.)

The same organizations met with the SDS staff during the second week in March, to propose that sponsorship be transferred to an Ad-Hoc Committee representing the established peace organizations. Though the Committee was to list only individuals, it was clear that they would function only as organizational representatives. The Ad-Hoc Committee would become the official sponsors of the March and make all decisions concerning it. The SDS staff, somewhat surprised, attempted to find out how far the proposed Ad-Hoc Committee would respect the definitions which SDS had articulated. The representatives of the various peace organizations, who had projected themselves as the Ad-Hoc Committee, pledged themselves willing to include left-wing student representation so long as a demand for representation did not make the Committee unworkable. The Committee accepted the placards which SDS had proposed, accepted SDS's official "call" for the March, and proposed only that the Ad-Hoc Committee circulate a second, shorter call, signed by adult peace leaders, to the non-student world. The members of the proposed Ad-Hoc Committee disagreed with the SDS definition of the March only on the issue of speakers, but here the disagreement was severe. SDS wanted speakers chosen from those groups in American society which might clearly oppose American foreign policy: the grass-roots civil rights movements, the urban poor, students, the professors organizing the proliferating "teach-ins," the "maverick" Senators and Representatives. The members of the proposed Ad-Hoc Committee wanted "name" speakers more conventionally acceptable —Dr. and Mrs. Martin Luther King were among their suggestions. No agreement was reached. Instead, the proposed Committee pledged to honor SDS's choice of speakers, but indicated that they would invite the additional speakers they felt were necessary and fitting.

The SDS staff explained to the proposed committee that the transferral of sponsorship would have to be accepted by the SDS National Council through a mail vote. Though individual SDS staff members told the committee that they felt the change in sponsorship would be accepted, they made it clear that nothing could be considered definite until the ballots were received and counted. But it was already the second week in March, little more than a month away from the appointed Saturday; the time necessary to send out and receive the ballots of the National Council would hamper the activities of the proposed Ad-Hoc Committee. So both the committee and the SDS staff decided to proceed as if the transfer of sponsorship had been approved. A. J. Muste wrote an adult "call," which was circulated to individuals prominent in the peace groups for their signature; a covering letter warned that the more inclusive sponsorship of the March became effective only upon approval

of the SDS National Council. Muste's call was circulated at
the same time that the SDS staff requested its National Council
to vote on the proposed transfer of sponsorship. The National
Office made no recommendation, but stated the arguments:
pro that organizational chauvinism should not take precedence
over a unified national protest in the face of the dangerous imme-
diacy of the war; con, that to turn the March over to a defunct
peace movement would compromise its message and destroy its
appeal to young people.

The votes came in slowly, but the final count showed that
a slim majority approved the change in sponsorship. However,
many votes stipulated conditions that could not be guaranteed
and many more were clearly ambivalent. The officers discussed
the results of the voting, considered the many objections to
the way the vote was conducted, the failure to arrange adequate
discussion and the extreme pressure of time and decided that
the National Council (and by implication, the entire organization) was far from agreeing that the change of sponsorship
should be made. Several officers who had voted Yes changed
their votes to No and the proposal was defeated.

When the SDS staff reported to the projected Ad-Hoc Committee that their proposal had been defeated, the March was
only four weeks away. The adult "call" had gone out and some
peace leaders felt that they had been tricked by a clever student
organization which had enlisted their aid but had intended,
all along, to deny them sponsorship and equal participation.

The animosity and resentment stirred by SDS's refusal to
transfer its sponsorship was one of the major causes for the
disaffiliation, enmity and attempts at sabotage of the March
by several peace leaders. Although a new letter went out to
everyone who had received the adult "call" informing them
that SDS would retain sole sponsorship of the March (but asking
for their support and endorsement), some of the adult peace
leaders were so provoked that they were actually talking and
working against the March.

During the final weeks of preparation, constant rumors
about opposition and dissension by heretofore respected members of the peace and radical communities drifted back to the
SDS office, but the staff was totally absorbed in the massive
and complex problems of organization and had neither the

time nor the energy to investigate the rumors. By early April most observers realized that the possibility of only a few hundred diehards to parade disconsolately before the White House was dim; enough trains and buses had been booked to send the estimates climbing towards 15,000. During those last weeks, several small incidents further provoked the various peace groups and provided the SDS staff with an accelerating index of the suspicion, distrust and anger felt by individuals within them.

The subway posters caused the first outburst. Large (46" x 30"), graphic (a head-and-torso profile of a little Vietnamese badly seared and scarred by napalm), and denunciatory ("WHY ARE WE BURNING, TORTURING, KILLING THE PEOPLE OF VIETNAM? . . . TO PREVENT FREE ELECTIONS"), the posters had been designed for SDS by Lee Baxandall (an editor of *Studies on the Left*) and Fred Gardner (an editor of *Scientific American*). While some SDS staff felt that they would have chosen a different wording or photograph, they decided to accept and use the several thousands posters provided. But many individuals, both at the League for Industrial Democracy and the various peace organizations, were furious; they felt the posters clearly implied that if America were to withdraw from South Vietnam, free elections would follow.

SDS was next attacked for aiding the transformation of the Vietnam march in the San Francisco area into a united front sponsoring activity "which is in fact more hostile to America than to war." The phrase is from Robert Pickus, Western area Turn Toward Peace director, quoted in a TTP press release announcing its dissociation from the San Francisco Bay Area Rally scheduled for the same day as the main protest in the Capital. SDS's National Office was so involved with work that the West Coast chapters had been advised to make their own decision about the form of supporting activity. Apparently the Berkeley (University of California) SDS chapter, the Women's Strike for Peace and the Berkeley DuBois Clubs were the key sponsoring groups for the Bay Area Rally and the plans and publicity for that rally indicated to Pickus "that the March would condemn American violence and ignore the use of violence by other forces in Vietnam." But when Western area TTP disassociated itself from the rally, not only the local SDS chapter, but the national organization was blamed for the increased "anti-Americanism" and "popular front" activity which many within the peace movements perceived in the last weeks before the March.

Several of the press releases issued by the SDS National Office also piqued and offended various adult peace leaders. Since SDS had retained sole sponsorship, it issued a constant stream of press releases as the demonstration date approached, without first having the releases inspected by individuals and groups supporting the March. One release argued that the SDS March would be a unique protest because it attempted to arouse an independent constituency not tied to the Administration; the release asserted that the March would be different from traditional American peace activity. After President Johnson's John Hopkins' speech on April 17, which committed America to continued bombing of North Vietnam while inviting unconditional negotiations with anyone except the National Liberation Front, a press release written by Tod Gitlin and Carl Oglesby accused the President of attempting "to con the American people." The peace group leaders were distressed at SDS's characterization of their dependent political position and their conventional activity and disturbed by what they considered an intemperate, tactless attack on President Johnson. And many claimed the right of inspection and consultation about SDS's press statements *before* they were issued, a right clearly reserved for sponsors rather than supporters. Though it appeared to many on the SDS staff that the peace leaders were trying to legitimate their protest and whittle down their outrage, it seems clear, in retrospect, that each "intemperate" and "tactless" utterance confirmed many peace leaders' fears that an anti-American coalition was shaping up.

That suspicion was reinforced by a songsheet distributed by the National Office. "Songs of Vietnam," a mimeographed sheet containing four familiar songs with new words by Todd Gitlin, Nanci Gitlin and Paul Potter, was sent out in an internal SDS mailing and had no connection with the March. Several individuals at Beekman Street saw the sheet and took violent exception to one chorus of a revised Freedom Song, with words by Tod Gitlin. The verse began with "No strategic hamlets, No strategic hamlets, No strategic hamlets around me." The offending chorus continued: "And before I'll be fenced in, I'll vote for Ho Chi Minh, Or go back to the North and be free." The line of argument which emerged from the furor asserted that there was no freedom under Ho Chi Minh in the North, and that unless SDS realized this and was prepared to assert the totalitarianism of North Vietnam and other Communist regimes, they were dangerously compromising the protest value of the Washington March.

The last week produced the final, divisive flurry of anti-March activity. On Wednesday night, April 14, the National Executive Committee of Turn Toward Peace met in New York City. The Committee read and discussed the statement of disassociation from the Bay Area Rally issued by Robert Pickus of Western Area TTP, recorded its sympathy with the Washington March, but added its "grave concern" about some of the endorsing organizations and the "tone, management, and message" of SDS's pre-March organizing activity. On Thursday, April 15, staff at SDS's National Office received phone calls from Senator Gruening and I. F. Stone. Gruening was worried about Communist infiltration; he had been warned of the possibility. Stone was worried that Gruening might decide not to speak to the marchers at the Sylvan Theater. SDS staff reassured both men that all plans and arrangements for the March and rally were firmly controlled by SDS members and staff.

On Thursday afternoon, at the home of Robert Gilmore, Executive Director of Turn Toward Peace, more than a dozen influential members of the peace and radical communities met to discuss the SDS March on Washington. According to A. J. Muste, interviewed by Jack Newfield (*Village Voice*, May 6, 1965), the meeting was called by Rustin, who wanted (as Newfield quotes Muste) "to torpedo the March because he thought communists had taken it over in some places." Though Rustin, according to Muste, wanted the group to issue a statement intended to cripple the March, the group, after long debate, issued a mild statement of sympathy that disagreed with the position of "some of the elements in the March," encouraged the possibility of a shift in American foreign policy as suggested in the President's Johns Hopkins' speech and welcomed the cooperation of all individuals "not committed to any form of totalitarianism" within the independent peace movement.

Norman Thomas, Muste, Rustin, H. Stuart Hughes and Gilmore were among the signers of this statement.

The press release containing the statement was issued Friday, the day before the March. Jack Smith (*National Guardian*, May 1) reported that "the statement was considered so urgent that it was delivered by hand to most of the city's daily newspapers and radio-TV stations." The most notable use made of it was the *New York Post's* editorial of April 17, the day of the March. "On the eve of this weekend's 'peace march' on Washington," the editorial begins, "several leaders of the peace movement have taken clear note of attempts to convert the event into a pro-Communist production." The editorial then summarizes the statement released by the group which met at Gilmore's house, lists the prominent signers, quotes the statement welcoming cooperation from non-totalitarian-minded individuals and groups and concludes with the warning that "there is no justification for transforming the march into a frenzied, one-sided anti-American show. Some of the banners advertised in advance are being carried to the wrong place at the wrong time."

After the March proved so huge and responsible a success, the meeting at Gilmore's house, and the statement which resulted, began to take on the same symbolic meaning as the attempt to force the MFDP to compromise at the Democratic Convention in Atlantic City. What seems clear is that those whose concern about a fancied threat of Communist control led them to attempt to wreck the March (Rustin and Gilmore) were in a minority at that meeting; the majority were somewhat concerned about the inclusion of groups like the DuBois Clubs and the May 2 Movement, but sympathetic to the March and its goals. A few who signed the statement because it was innocuous and they were unaware of the context are reported ready to repudiate their signatures. H. Stuart Hughes has already done so in a letter to Harvard SDS. A few participants left the meeting before it ended and discovered their signatures on a very different statement from the one they had expected. Moreover, not everyone present signed; Dave McReynolds and Ralph DiGia refused, and Dave Dellinger, editor of *Liberation* and one of the leaders of the pacifist movement, was not even invited.

There are also rumors about the genesis of the *Post's* editorial and the involvement of some of the signers in the *Post's* flat, Red-baiting statement about Communist attempts to subvert the March; it is not clear whether the *Post's* editorial writers offered their own conclusions or whether they were aided. But the charges and countercharges continue. In addition to Jack Smith's comprehensive account of the pressures brought to bear on the March and the Red-baiting involved and Jack Newfield's interview with A. J. Muste, Dave Dellinger's editorial in the May *Liberation,* "The March on Washington and its Critics," assesses the speeches at the March, the qualities of protest involved and then rehearses the efforts to wreck it. I. F. Stone's praise of the March, in his *Weekly* of April 26, includes a slap at the *Post* for being "stampeded by nervous adult peace leaders" into running its editorial. A memorandum from Mrs. Gardner Cox, Mrs. Anne Farnsworth and Martin Peretz to the signers of the April 16 statement expresses their distress and shock about the "efforts to undermine the March on Washington by people known as leaders of the peace movement." The memorandum argues that the statement indicated a "recrudescence of McCarthyism," accused the signers of lending their prestige "to a foolish, divisive and destructive tactic," accused Pickus of Red-baiting and defended the goals and conduct of the SDS March. Robert Gilmore's reply corrects some details but offers no defense. Staughton Lynd's open letter to Bayard Rustin (see below) has so far evoked no response.

The attempts to gain control of the March on Washington, and later to discredit it, like the attempts to force the MFDP to compromise at Atlantic City, illuminate the growing divergence between the new radicals and those still caught up in the ideological concerns of the old left and the strategies of realignment and coalitions at the top. The continued refusal of sections of the peace movement to work with overt Communist and left-wing groups, even within a protest activity sponsored and controlled by a non-Communist organization whose principles and activity all respected, indicates a steadily growing isolation of the traditional peace groups from the new student movements. The difficulty these organizations found in functioning as supporters rather than as sponsors of the

March grew out of this isolation and a concommitant ignorance of the extent and spirit of student alienation from the concerns of the Cold War.

Moratorium*

Jeremy Brecher

I

True mass movements develop quickly; they contain contradictory impulses; they change rapidly in the face of events their leaders cannot control. The great mass movement called the Moratorium already shows three explicit political strands, each with its own assumptions and its own trajectory for the movement.

1) For the great majority of participants, the Moratorium is essentially an expression of sentiment, based on the hope that such as expression will somehow sway the President to change his course. They show somewhat the touching spirit of the Russian peasants who demonstrated on Bloody Sunday, 1905, in the belief that if only the Czar knew the people's misery he would save them. In this case, however, faith is put not in the magical mantle of divine authority, but in the equally magical belief that 'the government represents the people' and therefore will act upon their will. A more sophisticated version maintains that politicians in a democracy must respond to public pressures; the example is given of Johnson's reversal of Vietnam policy in the face of overwhelming public pressure. But the fact is that even Johnson's extreme political isolation, which would have led to the fall of any parliamentary government in the world, led him only to make a change in strategy, while leaving half-a-million men in Vietnam.

To the extent that the Moratorium remains within this framework it has no future, for the October 15th demonstrations

---

* *Liberation*, December, 1969, 7—8. Reprinted with permission.

alone were enough to show overwhelming popular desire to get out of Vietnam, as did the October Gallup Poll showing that a bill to withdraw all U. S. troops from Vietnam by the end of 1970. was supported nearly two-to-one. If the Moratorium retains this view, it may grow for a month or two, but after that it will gradually fade away, leaving little effect on the actual course of events.

2) The second strand constitutes opposition politics. It is essentially a continuation of the Kennedy-McCarthy movement of 1968—even the faces are the same. It too is based on a touching faith in the electoral process, seemingly impervious to the results of experience. Its proponents have not learned the obvious lesson of the 1968 campaign: that the electoral process is controlled from above, not below. They have not learned the obvious lesson of the A.B.M. struggle: that the real power over governmental action does not lie in elected bodies. They have not noticed that Nixon ran as a 'Peace candidate,' as did our other Vietnam War Presidents, 'we seek no wider war' Johnson and 'let us put a truce to terror' Kennedy, before him.

Naturally, there are always politicians who are willing to associate themselves with 'peace' when peace is popular. Thus, for example, Teddy Kennedy and George McGovern both associated themselves with the Moratorium by speaking on October 15 —and proposed that all troops should be withdrawn by 1972! Several top Moratorium organizers themselves see it as a jumping-off point for their own political careers: Adam Walinsky, who all but took over the New York Moratorium office, is planning his campaign for state attorney-general, and Sam Brown, national director of the Moratorium, is talking about a Massachusetts congressional campaign.

The program of this approach will be to keep the Moratorium going for a few more months, then swing it into the 1970 primaries and elections, building a base for a McCarthy-style campaign in 1972. Its main requirements are that the movement remain respectable, give visible support and loyalty to likely candidates, and continue to grow for a few months until it can be channeled into electoral action.

3) The third strand is confrontation. In its extreme form, as practiced by Weatherman, it is rejected by most of the Moratorium movement, but as the legacy of the civil rights movement

and the old Mobilization Committee, its basic idea that 'power is in the streets' remains the frame of reference for most radicals in the peace movement. It assumes that each confrontation simultaneously advertises the radicals' cause and undermines the claim of the government to represent the popular will. If the government uses violence, it presumably de-legitimates itself further with the population by showing that the basis of its power is not consent but force. At some point in the escalation of demonstrations, the demonstrators (as Staughton Lynd once imagined it) simply march to the White House and in their overwhelming numbers take back control of the country.

The first problem with this approach is quite obvious—until the military and police power of the state dissolves, it is based on sheer fantasy. As the efforts to 'storm' the Pentagon in the October, 1967 Mobilization, the battles at the 1968 Democratic Convention, and the recent Weatherman demonstrations in Chicago show, such tactics are essentially suicidal; not only because of the direct effects of the state's brutality on demonstrators, but because few sane people deliberately offer themselves up as victims of police brutality where there is no other gain to be made. That is one reason why confrontation actions have had steadily fewer participants each time since the Pentagon demonstrations of 1967, even while opposition to the war grew by leaps and bounds.

The second problem is perhaps more important. The favorite tactic of an unpopular ruling group is to turn the sentiment of the population against the radical opposition. Since confrontation can always be interpreted as a deliberate provocation of violence, it plays directly into the hands of the authorities, who through their control of the press can make even a non-violent confrontation appear a deliberate act of violence. Even such flagrant official aggression as that of Daley's cops at the 1968 Democratic Convention was palmed off as 'demonstrators' violence' to a majority of the population. Thus, the prime political objective of confrontation fails; the government is permitted to portray itself as the bastion of public interest and public order under attack by a few violent malcontents. The radicals, desiring to show to the people their own power, reveal instead only the weakness of demonstrators before the military power of the state.

The program of the confrontationists will be primarily to

make the Moratorium demonstrations more 'militant'—that is, essentially to seek conflict with the police rather than to avoid it. If the Moratorium and Mobilization Committees do not adopt such a course, they will attempt to generate such confrontations through separate demonstrations and organizations. The result will be a tendency toward splitting of the movement, falling off of mass support, new vulnerability to governmental attack, and no doubt a few concussions.

II

All of these tendencies are rooted in the idea that real power lies in Washington. But the Moratorium movement also contains the seeds of a different approach.

Despite the apparent power of the men in Washington to make the crucial decisions, it is not they who keep the country going, who do its work and fight its wars. Rather, it is the people —the same people who support two-to-one the withdrawal of all U.S. troops from Vietnam. If they refuse to work—if they strike —the war must end. Indeed, the Moratorium itself was originally conceived as a general strike against the war, but was watered down by leaders who, as the New York *Times* put it, "liked the idea of political action but not the threat of a strike." To end the war, the Moratorium must more and more become a general strike against the war. It is here that the real power of the movement lies, not in playing politics or playing with violence.

Of course, a general strike does not come into being simply because some organization calls for it. It will only come about if public sentiment moves from a mere dislike of the war to a decision to force it to end, and if the movement puts its faith in itself, not in politicians who promise but won't—or can't— deliver. But as long as the government continues the war, the movement against it will grow and deepen, and the Moratorium will be able to take on more and more the character of a general strike.

Facing Up to Repression*

Rennie Davis

Two badges flash across some beefy fingers, too quick to see the identification numbers. "Officer Bell's my name. This here is Officer Luggio. We're assigned to you, Davis, as long as you're in town with these hippies and yippies. Make it easy on both of us, hear? We want the rundown on where you're going and coming and where you're staying, that's all. And I wouldn't try any fancy stuff at shaking us or anything like that. It'd make us look bad back at the district, and, mister, if you make us look bad, we're gonna have to make you look real bad...."

Here comes the ridiculous extreme of that American theory that reduces the demonstrators, riots and revolutions in the world to the work of the "outside agitator." Here is the actual man getting paid to show up and walk the streets behind the "leader" who is suspected for his travels state to state, stirring up civil disorders. The notorious troublemaker is pursued into the bathroom, down to the beach, over to the television studio, up to the doorstep of the bedroom and to any other spot where disruption or chaos might break out.

Living in the free world, it's somewhat easier to dismiss this intrusion into a man's life as a humorous accident. One can accept it graciously the way you accept a high school teacher or welfare caseworker. The government tail is friendly. He has his clever jokes ("Davis seems to like that Chinese food," one says, followed by great howls of laughter.) The tail looks after you in a world of constant danger. ("Our job is to protect you," he says. "A lot of people around here want you dead as a fucking door, you know. We want to make sure nothing mean happens to you. It's like you was President of the United States.") But, above all, the tail is a professional, a career man, carefully selected and trained by that developed American mind which reasons this country has no social problems, only "outside agitators," the same mind that figures the war in Vietnam can be won by assassinating 85,000 Viet Cong "leaders" (Operation Phoenix)

---

* *Liberation*, June, 1969, reprinted with permission.

or by sealing up the demilitarized zone to hold back the North Vietnamese "outsiders" (the McNamara wall).

Of course, it sometimes turns out that it's "Officer Bell" who wants you dead as a fucking door. One tail met me at the airport in Chicago and declared that if I would cooperate, he would protect me from his police partner who had a bullet in his pocket with my name on it. Once in Washington, D.C., I turned a corner with two tails behind me and decided to try a little run for it. When they turned the same corner and saw me about 50 yards ahead of them, galloping, one yelled, "Stop or I'll shoot." I stopped. The other partner tail then said, "No, no, that's not right." I got away with the mix-up about the orders of the day. Not too uncommon was the remark of one Chicago tail, during the Democratic Convention: "After this motherfucking protest, I'm gonna stomp you to death, fucking commie." Your average, local tail is about as much protection as facing a hail storm naked.

If you complain to the judge about the constant death threats by the police agent who follows you everywhere, the judge tells you to call the police. When the police headquarters are phoned, the man who answers never heard about "any tail assigned to you." So you go about your business with grown men, running their car bumper-to-bumper behind yours, following on foot everywhere you walk, waiting hours outside some office or house they think you are in. At the trial, the friendly tail turns unfriendly witness, stepping forward, swearing for the truth, and laying down this story that could come right out of Official Detective magazine. When you get into the courtroom, you stop wondering what the tail's about. The only question you have is, should we kill the tails or let them kill us?

With the first signs of tails, the first waves of indictments and serious prison sentences, the movement buzzes with the whisper of the word—repression. It's becoming The Worry of the movement and, at another level, it's the talk of the Justice Department, the center that will unleash whatever is to come. Some people have stopped working, they're so busy thinking about it all coming down. And Nixon's got a strategy that aims to bring it down. The outline of his plan is already apparent and is worth describing, for behind its double-barrel purpose lies the objective of not only "stopping the dissenters" but diverting public attention away from the war in Vietnam. The war needs more time to "win," according to the fantasies of the Pentagon. And another public issue could defuse the domestic pressures against continuing in Vietnam. That issue, packaged through the media as the campus disrupters and black power militants, is us. We are to be made the smokescreen that allows the war to go on.

Nixon's repression project is simple: mixing punishment, fear and cooptation. Part one is to "get the leaders." Even though everyone knows that the average "disrupter" hates leaders, doesn't have any, and depends on no one individual for his politics, direction, energy or passion, the TV-spawned spokesmen of the movement will be dragged into courts, indicted on vague charges of "inciting to mob action" or "conspiracy." Once these vile conspirators are shown to be behind the misguided conduct of America's youth, the government will dramatically expose that they are also agents of foreign enemy powers (someone made a trip to Cuba). There will be much publicity accompanying the judges' five-year sentences.

The second part of Nixon's assault will be the "outlawing" of the revolutionary organizations, especially the Black Panther Party and Students for a Democratic Society. The current police practice of gunning down Panthers in their communities will continue, along with the dramatic uncovering of "secret plots" to blow up white people. Panthers will also be indicted under the Smith Act, which makes it a crime to advocate the overthrow of the government. SDS will be the chief victim of the 1968 Anti-Riot Law which makes it a crime to travel interstate with the *intent* of fomenting a riot (a riot is two or more people who break a law). Regional travelers will be forced into penitentiaries for this crime of radical speech.

In addition, the current tactics of repression will be vastly accelerated: new state laws that prohibit any tactic that seems to be gaining effectiveness, congressional witch-hunt hearings, propaganda reports from various state and national investigatory commissions, police spy infiltration, an unending procession of grand jury investigations, court injunctions, FBI visits to the homes of parents, police raids on movement offices, more tails, more mace, more expulsions, subpoenas and convictions. And when mace and clubs aren't enough, they will bring out the shotguns and shoot us, as Reagan has done.

Nixon's plan is to isolate and crush the "hard-core," to frighten the "idealists," and to add some social change that shows the infinite flexibility and reasonableness of American capitalism (abolish the draft; perhaps legalize marijuana).

The mere mention of these plans is enough to shake some people out of the movement. Others joke about it, these signs of our future, the constant threats, the phone calls that say "your time has come, commie," the police pledges to put someone away permanently. Most radicals are continuing their work as before, while around the country, our offices are installing new security devices, doors are bolted, shot guns are purchased and hung in back closets, strangers are frisked for weapons at the door. As the official tolerance of radicals narrows and our threat to the power structure becomes more serious, we will require a strategy of defense consistent with long-term political objectives and based on the principles of self-defense, a definition of the enemy, a class analysis of the repressive apparatus designed to keep us in line, support for defense based on coalition rather than a narrowing circle of political friends, survival and a clear articulation of the politics behind our "crime." Above all, a defense must not be isolated from ongoing activities of the movement. It must be made into an integral part of organizing and education in the community.

When I traveled to North Vietnam in the Fall of 1967, the Vietnamese I met talked little about war atrocities. They did not parade before me victims of napalm and anti-personnel bombs. I had to seek out these people and their personal stories. The Vietnamese wanted Americans to know of their problems and successes in building a new society underneath the bombs—the underground schools and hospitals, the road brigades and women's liberation groups, the agricultural cooperatives, and village self-defense units. Their preoccupation was with organizing a people's revolution, not with "the repression" visited upon them by the U.S. Air Force. Repression is not the issue, and any movement that pushes its own defense to the center loses.

Our defense must begin with educating people to the idea of self-defense, that against attacks on our persons or organizations, we have the right to defend ourselves. The frontline danger to the most radical groups in the country are police and the growing American right wing, particularly its para-military operation, the Minutemen. The assassination attempt on Herbert Aptheker in 1967, the abortive attacks on the pacifist encampments at Voluntown, Conn., Wingdale, N.Y. and Camp Midvale in New Jersey, the thousands of names compiled on lists marked for death, the stockpiling of arms in underground bunkers and the active experimentation in chemical-biological warfare research by a national underground network of superpatriots makes the Minutemen a serious source of future trouble. People are inclined to understand self-defense only after a friend like Dick Flacks has been nearly killed sitting in his university office. Then it is too late.

A defense strategy requires definition of the enemy, the idea that there is a complex of forces dangerous to the movement. People think they can "educate" the FBI agent who drops around for a conversation or that the innocence of a friend can be explained to the star chamber grand jury. Again and again, such people unwittingly help lay the basis for the indictment. There is no agency of the government with which we should cooperate (though certain outfits like HUAC may be turned into a public forum to demonstrate our contempt for such committees).

A defense strategy must teach people that law is an instrument for repression rather than justice. You never hear of the case of a supermarket owner being clubbed by a cop for overcharging his customer or federal marshals rushing into the White House to arrest a President for the murder of Vietnamese. My own judge in the case of the federal indictment stemming from convention week is a 74-year-old man, tied to a corporation engaged in weapon production for Vietnam. He is expected to pass judgement on young people whose "crime" includes militant opposition to the war. A man who has the financial ability to buy his way into the judgeship, a man who has an immediate dislike for those he must judge, should be condemned along with the system of injustice for which he stands.

Defense must not serve the enemy's purpose of isolating us from the people. If possible, defense should appeal to an even broader constituency than the act of speech or program that brought on the attack. We don't have to "water-down our politics" to appeal to the liberals or uncommitted workers. But we ought to develop many tactics in a board defense strategy that permits support from a variety of political constituencies. I do not expect liberals to support the politics of the eight defendants in the conspiracy trial. They will not like the content of the trial. But I would defend active involvement of any group that wants to work against the unconstitutional Anti-Riot law or Smith Act. A court defense includes many aspects: education, fund-raising, legal preparation, the issue of civil liberties, the politics of the defendants, self-defense, etc. Through a creative variety of defense tactics, we can attract new people to the movement.

Not every court case can be turned into a "political" trial where one addresses himself to the outside community rather than to the capitalist judge. In some cases, there is little or no public interest. The movement is not capable of generating that interest. The issues involved have no fundamental principle that must be defended. Survival is the only issue at stake.

At other times, however, a trial offers the opportunity of a large public forum, an unfolding drama in which many people are participating and others are curiously watching to learn some of our purposes. Huey Newton's trial, for instance, succeeded in arousing a sympathetic and often militant public response. Such trials insure the movement's survival and promote its growth.

In our conspiracy trial in Chicago, we hope to turn the courtroom into a schoolhouse for the nation. The government wants to show that it was our intention to foment a riot in Chicago. We're going to show that conspiracies of small groups are not the cause of the popular opposition growing in America. The government will not find a handful of people responsible for riots, demonstrations, or protest of any variety. Only real problems and conditions of oppression move people to demand change and to struggle for it.

As the government becomes more repressive in its attempt to maintain order and to divert attention away from the war, as more military bases are put under lock and key to prevent troops from having contact with the anti-war movement, as more stockade rebellions occur, as expulsions from universities for political activity begin to reach the tens of thousands, the number of people who are willing to support insurrection will grow. I use the word insurrection deliberately. Our power no longer exists to soften public opinion. It exists in making people understand that to the men who rule this Empire, public opinion is a commodity to be manipulated, a weather vane of potential disaster to be read and measured, but hardly a force to be heeded. The force that they fear is the force of insurrection, the large scale active disregard of the repressive apparatus that has been created to keep people in line. That is our best defense.

Rennie Davis, a long-time movement activist, was among the eight indicted for conspiring to "incite riot" at the Democratic Convention last summer.

B. The Organization of the Powerless: The Experiences of the New Left with the Poor and on the Campus.

Accompanying protest, but itself beyond protest, the New Left has been largely concerned with the problems of organization. Yet before the end of the 1960's the New Left was dismissed for its apparent failure to be effective in the community and for its withdrawal into the sanctuary of the college campus. If we examine carefully the statements in this section, it becomes clear, however, that the battle is the same whether on or off the campus.

The years 1964-65 saw attempts by SDS to organize the poor. Their organizers worked in Chicago, Cleveland, Newark and Oakland, to name just a few cities. As Tod Gitlin describes it in the following section, the plan was first to organize the poor at a local level, then tie the local structures into a natural organization.

By 1966, most of these drives had failed, perhaps for the reasons discussed by Gitlin and which underlie Mario Savio's now famous speech, "An End To History."

The articles by Gitlin and Savio suggest that perhaps the withdrawal onto the campuses was not so much a retreat as a revivification for the Left. This theme will be explored more fully in the concluding chapter.

The Radical Potential of the Poor*

Tod Gitlin

The radical experience in organizing the poor has been as misunderstood as it has been brief. Often organizers have not spoken clearly to criticisms from within as well as without, though for good reason—the premium has been on organizing the poor, testing some principles, not embroidering a theory somebody else might someday apply. As a result the theory of this new work—implicit and explicit—has been written mostly by those who would caricature it to suit their own political slants, sympathetic or not. And as some of the early projects collapsed, there has also been something of a crisis in confidence among radical organizers grappling for ways to make sense of a complex and exhausting experience. Clarity about what has and has not been done has become not just a matter of courtesy to critics, but of balance and survival for present and prospective organizers.

Why organize? At first, as SDS people and others moved into poor communities in 1964, the main ideas were there: In a system that satisfies many needs for most Americans, the poor are still demonstrably in need—and know it. They are also less tied to the dominant values, just as—and partly because —they are less central to the economy that creates and expresses those values. They have a certain permanence necessary for a sustained movement. Though a minority, they are a substantial minority. They exhibit a potential for movement— for understanding their situation, breaking loose, and committing themselves to a radical alternative.

Those beliefs are basic, and basically valid. But at this juncture the purposes of radical organizing projects can be listed more precisely, even at the risk of drawing artificial distinctions:

---

* Reprinted with permission from The International Socialist Journal, v. 24; no. 24.

First, to enable the most powerless people to get a handle on the decisions and non-decisions, now made *for* them, that debase and deform their lives. Second, to help the poor get more of the material goods and services prerequisite to a decent life. Third, to undergird serious proposals for the humane extension of the welfare state, and keep them responsive to the needs of those "for whom" they are proposed and granted. Fourth, to help maintain momentum for a Negro movement in need of reliable allies.

Fifth, to raise, insistently, in poor communities and at every level outside, these issues, among many: who runs the society, and in whose interest? Who is competent to make which decisions for the poor, or for anyone? Who is "for" the poor? what do the poor "need"? how tolerant is America? how in America do people get what they want? how do they want what they "want"? what happens when people govern themselves? what institutional changes would make a difference? Sixth, to strengthen the poor as a source and reservoir of opposition to the final rationalization of the American system: to keep the country open to authentically different values and styles.

Seventh, to galvanize students, professionals, and others into durable confrontations with the ethos and structure of the society; and to lend urgency and values to parallel movements. Eighth, to amass pressure for public, domestic spending, and thus, in political effect, against an aggressive foreign policy.

And ninth, to plant seeds that might grow into the core of a mass radical movement sufficiently large and serious and conscious and strategically placed to transform American institutions.

How are these objectives practical, and how are they compatible? Provisional answers might be found in the experience of two "community unions" seeded by SDS-JOIN in a mostly Southern-white neighborhood of Chicago, and the Newark Community Union" Project (NCUP) in a black ghetto.

Issue-organizing

The underclass has its most abrasive contacts with the ruling elites less at the point of production than outside it. Bad housing, meager and degrading "welfare," destructive urban renewal, vicious police, hostile and irrelevant schools, inadequate community facilities (hospitals, nurseries, traffic lights, parks, etc.) are the general rule and are felt as a pattern of victimization above and beyond each of these separate issues. The job of the organizer is to find those people most aroused by felt grievances; to organize, with them, action on those issues; to amplify the feeling that these are common, *caused* problems, not individual faults, accidents or exceptions; to build through tangibly successful action a confidence in the weight of collective action, and to discover and teach through failures the limits of present capabilities and the work that lies ahead. The more engaged and mature the organization, the more "success" or "failure" becomes the subtle estimate of organizer and organized as they begin to see "the problem" as larger, more complex than before. In this new context, gradually, success comes to mean both the achievement of specific change (getting a landlord to make repairs, winning a welfare right, etc.) and the commitment of a resident to participate in the project's work. Organization on any single issue may span only a few individuals (welfare rights) or a block (traffic light) or the entire neighborhood or city (police, urban renewal). The smaller the unit, the easier a visible victory.

As the action on one issue runs its course—through meetings, pickets, confrontations with city officials, etc.—many of the people involved drop away; most to become passive supporters, some to become critics. Some get more involved and decide to stick with it. They generate, discover, happen upon, are asked to consider further issues—thus, more actions, further discoveries, new people, and so on. The model is an amoeba. The nuclei are a hard-core of people attracted by one campaign, or by the notion of fundamental change in the neighborhood or city or country or by the novelty and spirit of the project; slowly and with difficulty they carve out a place in the protoorganization. Its motion is compounded of *purpose* (to attain what seems central in most people's lives, or to draw in new groups of people—"building the organization"—or to achieve visible change, or to generate issues of control and social structure, or to maintain the community itself against outside pressures), *circumvention* (what cannot be tackled at *this* level of organization), and *randomness* (who shows up, wanting what done).

Long dead is any speculation that any one issue will be the key to unlock the local structure of power, let alone the national one. When SDS first sent students into poor communities in 1963–64 there was a strong feeling that the issue of jobs or income might be a single decisive lever of change, a feeling based on some naïve expectations about the pace and effect of automation. JOIN, the first organizing venture, stood for "Jobs or Income Now." During the course of the summer of 1964, some organizers argued that white unemployment was far too little and diffused (in Chicago, at any rate) to be the basis for organization; moreover, that jobs or income were too remote as early demands. They proposed instead an emphasis on smaller, neighborhood demands more easily won. The debate was jocularly summarized as one between "JOIN" and "GROIN" ("Garbage Removal or Income Now"). GROIN prevailed (NCUP had been GROIN from the start), and the JOIN office was relocated that fall in the uptown neighborhood, the largest concentration of poor whites in the city, as JOIN Community Union.

Issues are connected through argument as well as experience so that the common elements of powerlessness and exploitation take on a new concreteness. As a prerequisite, the organization must concern itself with a span of issues (the jargon is "multi-issue"), not confine itself to one or two alone. In this way it reaches a greater variety of people, generates a feel for the relatedness of issues, binds different types of people together, and lessens the chance that success or failure on any one issue will determine the fate of the budding movement. This openness toward issues leaves the organization free to take advantage of new situations, new grievances, new moods as they arise. But the danger of a multi-issue organization is that as it grows, it might spin off so many issues, each with its own work-force and constituency, that "the center cannot hold." The centrifugal force swells (paradoxically) as the organization becomes more solid—as community people become more confident, gain organizational skills, take on pieces of work genuinely their own. At such peaks, many of the pent-up envies, aggressions, and cupidities this society bestows on its victims are likely to burst out. Cohesion, the stuff of permanence, then depends in part on a rhythm of activities, in part on the level of good feeling, and on the ideological and symbolic identity built up over a period of time. (Ideally there should probably be cycles of activity, periods of disparate projects alternating with times when a single activity will involve the entire organization.)

The special quality of *radical* issue-organizing is the intertwining of two different kinds of demands: demands for tangible concessions, which can be granted by existing institutions, and demands for control and substantial restructuring of those institutions. It is too early to say when the first kind of demands will be met; results have something to do with the elite embarrassment that would be caused otherwise, the legitimacy of the demand as measured by prevailing standards (e.g., pressure for a welfare right provided in law), the economic power that can be massed (e.g., rent strikes), the institution's best judgment of how to thwart the movement's growth ("unearned" concessions). The second kind can be thought of as transcendent, "utopian" demands, not capable of being met on the neighborhood or even the city level. These are demands that touch on the structure of authority, the question of legitimate power. They are tinged—locally and nationally—with a certain absurd pathos; the bravado of the powerless telling the powerful to disband because they are illegitimate, because they have no right to decide, because they have botched the job and must move aside. At the extreme, the placing of demands blurs into "challenge and disruption," because an institution will not agree to its wholesale destruction, and the movement lacks the strength to force it. But the radical insistence does not degenerate into "speaking truth to power" when it keeps the powerful on the defensive, exorts more and more concessions while diluting the agencies' legitimacy in the community—all of which are possible as the organization grows and community people become more comfortable making demands that will not be granted tomorrow.

In fact limitations of experience may lead us to overestimate the concrete futility of both material and structural demands on the local level. Certain of the structural demands could only be met through national and state legislation (e.g., that welfare recipients administer the welfare program), but others, in theory at any rate, could be won locally if pressure is "strong enough." (Organizers learn to guess at the chances for victory, but revise their guesses in the process of working toward a goal.) Those demands could be achieved without a massive shuffling of resources; their common motif is *autonomy;* they should be thought of as middle-range possibilities, lodged between the demands of the moment and a thoroughgoing reconstruction. For example, there seems to be intrinsic reason why the New York City Board of Education could not grant the right of parents to control Intermediate School 201; it would threaten their legitimacy to be sure, but might be the easiest way out if the parents' movement were deep and relentless enough. Likewise, the demand that the people affected by urban renewal dominate planning for their community, and be granted the resources (information, planners, money) to do so, does indeed require "a whole revision of the operation, a revision unimaginable without structural changes in the urban renewal agencies, and finally, subordination of the land-use cycle, and of contractual developers, to local initiative and control." What is *not* yet clear is that this goal, even when seen in its radical light, is impractical. There have been some few occasions when community organizations (not community unions) have turned urban renewal to their own uses, a result tantamount to curbing the violence of the land-use-cycle. A victory is *conceivable* if not imminent, and might spread to other neighborhoods and critics. Similarly, groups may decide that the police cannot be pressured politely through civilian review boards, but must be contained and rendered illegitimate if brutality is to stop. The objective would not be to change police policy at the top, but to watch and challenge the occupiers so closely that they decide finally to let the community govern itself. Difficult as this would prove, it still seems more practical than the centralist approach, and could not be less effective in curbing terror than the showpiece review boards. Victories of the sort—"a whole lot of lettin' alone," as one JOIN member put it—would also illustrate and refine certain tensions in the concept of participatory democracy. Control over a local institution in a vacuum may inspire opposed groups to control *theirs* (though rightwing and other middle-class groups are likely to have that control already); it may also detract from efforts to change the larger structures and win new resources. Parents' control over I.S. 201 alone would leave the rest of New York's educational machine untouched, and so on for each of the other victories. The gamble of a community union, then, is that its local successes and strategies can be communicated as models for other groups and organizers to copy, and that its own people are firm enough in their direction to use the victory for momentum, not coasting or cooptation. This implacibility may be as much a matter of education and consciousness of "objective conditions."

Not so ironically, the strength of national and local systems of authority has been in their flexibility with regard to all aspects but the most central: private property is still sacrosanct but local control is a prevailing rhetoric whose limits are yet to be tested and extended. A victory on the city-wide level for the right of welfare recipients to organize "at the point of distribution" (the welfare office), conceivable in a city like Chicago in the foreseeable future, would not provide control over a central social structure, but would open up space for contact, organizing, and influence. Thus even at the level of the city, structural goals are not entirely utopian, and material goals are unevenly possible; the upshot might be a basis for natural expansion in the neighborhood and city; not fundamental change in structure or resources, but preconditions for and intimations of both. Material and structural victories even at the national level—abolition of stringent welfare regulations, guaranteed income, democratization of urban renewal—become at least imaginable as community unions sink roots and demonstrate, level by level, what can be done. But each step is agony.

Democracy and Durability

The community union seeks to become permanent without freezing. There is a long beginning stretch when residents are reached, temporarily involved, and then fade back into their personal lives and a passive sort of support. As some fall away there is renewed pressure to find others. If the organizer wades through the early frustrations, he is likely to find people who will stick. As they show interest, pieces of manageable work can be divided between the ex-students and the recruits. Something like a formal division of labor develops, through which people usually considered incompetent and inept find their own capabilities and make new ones. In both Newark and Chicago, community people have been taken on staff and play crucial roles. "Roles" are rather loosely defined to permit choice, but structured sufficiently to achieve specific aims (an issue-project, reaching new people, managing the office, research, fundraising, etc.). Roles are also set up to reflect varying levels of commitment: in JOIN there are full-time staff and a network of "stewards"—part-time contacts and organizers who relay problems to the central office, distribute newsletters, suggest and join in activities, and provide feedback; and then the wider span of members. Every so often all the levels come together for mass meetings, large actions, movies, skits, parties. The organization then has roots as well as a conscious thrust.

The mood of informality appeals to some community people, but confuses and alienates others; for most, at the beginning, a meeting means a time to dress up and listen quietly, though new people discover that it is easy to get up and talk. Community unions have moved from the dogmatic anarchism which some critics observed to be the pathology of the middle-class organizer. In JOIN at least there are formal leaders elected by an organizing committee (the staff and the most active people) and the membership as a whole. Offices rotate every month so that the skills and experience that come with nominal authority and the spokesman role can be spread, and power kept close to the source. (Among chairmen of the JOIN organizing committee have been day-laborers, an ex-hairdresser, a junkie ex-con, a fired building manager, a preacher without pulpit, a go-go dancer, a teenage "tough," and welfare recipients.) Meetings are freewheeling, sometimes baroque, but capable of making decisions. What emerges through those formal functions as well as through discussions, actions, and symbols is an identity that bears some relation to the community style. (What is hard is blending that style with the demands of decision-making; results are uneven.) Thus there is a hillbilly cast to JOIN songs—mostly adapted from Baptist hymns, some from civil rights anthems—reflecting the dominant population and culture, though most of the active hillbillies in JOIN do not exert formal policy influence in meetings. But then policy emerges mostly from an interplay among organizers' ideology, people's readiness to move, and mutual perceptions of the situation; it only surfaces at official meetings.

The experience in JOIN is that a working mesh of formal democracy and decentralized work is possible, but that it takes the most excruciating patience. Trust is established slowly and delicately, as organizers prove that action can get results, and make explicit their commitment to stay until, by general consent, it is time to get to work elsewhere. Organizers must ride what seems to be a recurrent cycle of turnover and crisis. After several ways of turnover, as the organization seems more stable, emphasis shifts to equipping the people who have committed themselves. Organizers perceive crisis: they have made now organizers, stabilized the organization, but have stopped reaching the unreached. They resolve, after much talk, to plunge outward again. Then relative stability tests the ability of organizers to make room for new people, and repeat the process. It is a tension built into the organizing aproach. Understood that way, it can be the project's greatest strength, its propulsion. Misperceived as failure, it become a self-fulfilling gloom.

What I mean to say is that as it grows the project aims, in a complicated way, to embody and symbolize and prove the possibility of a democratic society. It is somewhat like, but more complex than, the "live-in" conceived by Staughton Lynd:

> The spirit of a community, as opposed to an organization, is not, We are together to accomplish this or that end, but, We are together to face together whatever life brings. . . . The spiritual unity of the group is more important than any external accomplishment . . . the building of a brotherly way of life even in the jaws of Leviathan.

For as the project forges the idea of shared decision-making in a political community, it is also constantly pushing outward, its fraternity testing the outside world, challenging and disrupting it, creating and seeking openings, looking to replicate itself; and it is also prepared to risk its satisfaction for the rude receptions it is likely to get when it ventures outside. There is *restless community,* "something of our own" that dares its own exclusiveness, that thrives insofar as it sets itself problematic goals, that foregoes certainties as it constantly probes for a momentum of changes. By taking risks it avoids stasis and cynicism, the final victories of a society closing in. To the degree that Fruchter and Kramer are right about the closure and containment of tangible radical possibilities—and I am not yet judging the likelihood—their conclusions hold up:

> In an environment where the possibilities for fundamental change are obscure, where even the desire for change based upon assumptions different from those of the society presents itself as either irrational or pathological, there is a continuous pressure toward finding ways to "separate" from the society. The negation of the status quo in theory, language, acts, lacking any focus that would make change a real possibility, is always driven to seem partially utopian.

But while such despair is natural, it goes too far to say that "at the present time there is no adequate way of formulating this idea of existing 'outside' that does not over-emphasize utopian tendencies." The problem is rather, having formulated the idea, to make it work.

The project must resist the temptation to cut itself off from the whole society. The dangers are most acutely those of sectarian politics, apolitical posturing and the cultivation of relations with middle-class groups, and the powers that be at the expense of roots in the community. The project must continue to find in the culture of poverty at least a culture of resistance, and remain engaged with the sources of that resistance. It must replenish those sources and embody them in a *political* resistance, facing outward from the project. It must challenge the dominant trends and oppressive structures while challenging itself to refuse to take the future for granted. When the organizer despairs he may find solace in marveling at the community he has helped forge; but that is a fragile and short-lived pleasure. If he is to survive and work, he must again grow restless, and his beloved community must keep itself on the firing line.

The Education of Radicals

The education goal in a radical project is sometimes called "radical consciousness," which incorporates analysis, technique, information, and ideology, and is more than the sum of them. The means are "experience" and "teaching."

The organizing process itself is rich with usable experience. As people are brought into the project, their pre-existing populism is nurtured and made explicit. The organizer is constantly trying, as directly as possible, to dramatize the basic validity of that populism, clarifying its images of targets and allies, while challenging its destructive stereotypes (like white supremacy). Experience can provoke two sorts of lessons: discoveries about the common situation of separate groups of poor people (blocks, neighborhoods, races, regions, countries), and deepening sense of the structure of the society. People are not babied by being fed through different learning situations in measured stages; rather there is a dynamic which teaches us from the experience at hand. Almost any grievance or the most casual political remark can be lent a radical meaning. Given a certain forward motion either "success" or "failure" can teach; in the early stages especially, a certain proportion of "successes" is crucial.

It is true enough, as some Marxists point out, that poor people's experience with the political-corporate system is located mostly at the level of neighborhood issues, not directly with capitalists. The too-quick conclusion is that poor people—more than workers—are prevented from understanding capitalism. But, as Fruchter and Kramer insist, it stretches the point to pose an iron law of consciousness,

> posing a traditional form of exploitation as the only experience which yields an accurate analysis of capitalist structure, as if similar analysis was not possible from the starting-point of slum-ownership or the administration of welfare.... It may be that there is no hierarchy of necessary experience which yields selectively different levels of structural perception; in this tightly knit political economy, the analysis of any specific dehumanizing process, whether primary (class exploitation) or secondary (authority and control, resource distribution) contradictions, may lead one to an adequate structural perception of imperialist monopoly capitalism.

Propped by a unifying ideology of free enterprise, nationalism, and law and order, the class-consciousness of the well-fed
worker, blue- or white-collar, is limited by his relative prosperity: that of the slum-dweller, by his contacts with city
bureaucracies and the shifting middle class. But the poor are
probably still better equipped to understand—and find *new* ways
of understanding—the class structure of American society than
are most organized workers. The poor, benefiting less from
America's world position, are more open to radical views of
foreign policy. They may have more trouble discriminating between a political machine and its corporate backers, between a
public bureaucracy and the economic system; but the experience
of fighting urban renewal tends to draw the lines vividly—for
"students" as well. Anyway, while the phrase "imperialist
monopoly capitalism" is rich with meaning, a grasp of its lines
of authority and its operations simply does not flow directly out
of *anyone's* experience. One cannot demand of poor people what
one would want of no one else—the abandonment of debate
over the makeup and dynamic of the American system; not at
the early stage. The risks of intellectual flexibility, given some
elementary components of a radical view, seem to me less than
the power of sharp, visible intellectual conflict. It makes for
radical thinkers, not quoters of political theology.

But the organizer needs no excuses for using ideology to
clarify targets, to enrich and sharpen experience and supplement it as well. Ideology is not flaunted as a text but elaborated
as organizers work with residents: it flows through ordinary
conversion—the daily business of the staff—and through more
self-conscious structures. As the community union becomes
more solid, the formal methods of education become more fea-
sible. Thus, after two years of painfully slow organizing, JOIN
started a school for committed community people, where questions of class, power, social structure, American history and
foreign policy are raised through specially prepared pamphlets,
films, discussion, and role-playing. Far from resenting such
mind work, these people are wildly enthusiastic; having become organizers through the issue-movement process, they want
bearings in the world they hope to change.

Though the ability to communicate radical views of the
world is no substitute for movement and drive, it should not be

underestimated. OEO community action people, by contrast, cannot fail to notice that the Vietnam war erodes the resources of the "war on poverty," but the insight stops there. They demand, then, simply that the foreign war not be allowed to hinder the "war" at home. But in a community union people can and do demand of officials that they must end the war in order to make concessions, as well as for its own sake. The radical demand also renders the moderate one less risky, and is no more ineffectual; equally important, it tells the truth, moving past the idea that the President has just made a "mistake." On its face the radical demand cannot be met—not on the local level anyhow—but raising it is the key to the radical approach. In the same way, while the draft looms large in the lives of young men who are poor, to confront it immediately might be suicidal. Yet JOIN organizers have been able to broach the issue, gradually, with young Southern men who were first drawn into a movement against police brutality—not sidetracking their primary concern with police, but working from it to more general ideas about authority and violence. Consequently, a slowly widening circle of people think it legitimate to talk about proscribed issues. As the limits of permissible debate are extended, some people fall away, but the losses are tolerable. And those who agree to learn and argue seem to become more serious, rather than discouraged, as they appreciate the dimensions of tolerable controversy.

Radical education does not justify itself solely in its intrinsic worth. In the end, built on and reinforcing an open, democratic, and aggressive movement, the values and ideas crystallized by radical organizers are also the best protections against cooptation into liberal structures and ordinary reforms. Not that radical consciousness, God knows, will always suffice; as liberal mechanisms bloom and become more sophisticated, the temptations will grow to rest satisfied, to drown in neocolonial projects because they are "real," to decide that structure demands are after all peripheral, to sacrifice the "dogma" that ordinary people must participate in the major decisions. Right now, between the political price T.W.O. paid for minimal urban renewal concessions and the refusal of JOIN to pay that price (even for more substantial concessions, short of community say-so) there is much more than a marginal difference. To sustain that sort of difference if the stakes pile up, *without growing indifferent to needs,* will be a delicate and agonizing job. Radical organizers have yet to face the dramatic and decisive test of building a radical, catalytic movement of poor people while a triumphant coalition of modernizers and liberals is setting to work. While that event seems remote right now, it could develop in five or ten years on the backs of poor people's movements. How radicals would fare then—to the extent our planning matters—is more a function of how we organize than after it; how we exist "outside" while making raids on the "inside"; how we learn to "keep our eyes on the prize." So far, people in JOIN and NCUP have usually been able to resist the varied blandishments—substantive and stylistic—of modernizing elites without sacrificing access to visible accomplishments, and have been able to move into potentially "effective" but spongy structures without foundering. The risk is probably not so much that leaders will be brainwashed and bought by liberal structures as that they will be more gently tamed, "socialized," convinced that bureaucratic rationality is basically healthy and radical challenges and new styles "childish"—until finally the disruptive ideas and associations become uncomfortable, and victories become defeats. As this happens, organizers will have to learn to see a few people go, and return to work finding new people to keep up pressure on the liberal structures from the bottom. Against the authority of approved ways of doing things there are no guarantees in anyone's strategy; but there are safeguards available that have so far stood the test, and kept radical alternatives alive and on the offensive.

Counter-institutions and Catalysis

In the here and now there are a range of needs which orthodox political organizing cannot fulfill. For these purposes "counter-institutions" of different sorts have been conceived, and some set in motion. What they share in common is the attempt to "initiate the unorganized into the experience of self-government," to gain the justified allegiance of the community, and to extend the model of a democratic and accessible movement farther into the world of concrete needs. All the different types of counter-structures depend on a pre-existing level of organization and a shared sense of their intermediate positions—less than revolutionary, more than therapeutic. To propel and not stall the movement that gives rise to them, they must represent "something of our own" in tension with what is not, but should be. Erected prematurely they will devolve into bureaucracy, not self-government, and as centrifugal features drain energy from the rock-bottom work of organizing. It is a subtle business to judge when to start.

At one level are *economic counter-institutions* that meet urgent material needs for the community and, within it, for the movement, when the larger society cannot be forced to yield. Credit unions and job consumer cooperatives can make some jobs for organizers while filling wider needs. But even these efforts, small as they seem when set against the size of those needs, usually require more than the project's own resources. Southern "tent cities" organized by local SNCC groups to house displaced sharecroppers encounter the same trouble. Once there is a roof over people's heads there remains the need to raise thousands of dollars to capitalize a brick factory— to build homes while providing jobs. When public funds are precluded, these sorts of counter-institutions are forced to depend at first on fund-raising from liberal foundations and individuals. With rare exceptions, even if those sources do not want to impose conditions, their rules and values may require a timetable (like amortization within a very short time) or a certain accounting procedure that badly strains the possibility of structural innovation, the training and participation of local people. The project, organizers and residents together, must judge whether it can meet the conditions implied without sacrificing its identity; and then balance the sacrifice against the need. (It would be mistaken to judge in advance that residents will always be more malleable than "students," though that will usually and naturally be the case.) Then, once conditions can be accepted, the larger pressures of the society begin to operate: a monopolistic market squeezing producers' co-ops, various economic and political arrangements (bank-induced legislation, licensing, etc.) militating against credit unions and consumers' co-ops. Some job co-ops in the Southern movement have survived by carving out markets among sympathetic

Northerners and—more important for the spread of the movement—among local people. But the movement had to be solid
enough first to make a market for "movement producers"
among "movement people." Tom Hayden proposed a few years
back that Southern farm coops might be linked to Northern
poor people's at some take-off stage of organization which would
allow Northern and Southern groups to conceive the need,
meet and discuss the possibilities. While all such schemes should
be explored, and their limits are nowhere near reached, most
radical organizers see them as stop-gaps and tools of organization, not ends in themselves.

Yet there are times when to sustain momentum and self-
determination a community union will try to set up something
itself rather than demand it of authorities. There are no set
rules; rather there is a rhythm of approaches which can only
be judged by the standards of a particular project at a particular time. The issue then is not whether the government *ought*
to force companies to pay day-laborers the union scale rather
than $1.25 an hour (of course it ought to). The question be-
comes: *At this point in time* should JOIN invest energy in
lobbying for minimum wage extension and state-run employment offices, or should it try to get money to set up its own
non-profit day-labor agency? Should JOIN bargain with the
alderman to turn a parking lot into a playground, or try to set
up the playground itself? In the first case JOIN tried—unsuc-
cessfully—to get OEO money for its own agency, discourag-
ing some members who had worked hard on the proposal and
wanted to run the agency. (Thus the risk of aiming for the
counter-institution without the power to produce it.) In the
second, JOIN organized a mock election of kids in favor of
the playground and recruited middle-class help in convincing
the owner to turn over his land; it turned out JOIN was too
weak to find people to build and maintain the playground; but
more than a year after the "election," when OEO workers built
a playground on another lot on the block, residents promptly
dubbed it "the JOIN playground." (Even a premature "success" can force a small change and spread a reputation for
effectiveness.) At most, counter-institutional tactics may bring
a spiral of results; strength for the organization, pressure for

top-down change, and popular participation in both means and goal. Ordinarily, though, success will mean parks and stop signs, not new housing.

At a second level are *counter-institutions of culture and information*. JOIN's newspaper, *The Firing Line*, circulates 4,000 copies a week in the neighborhood and is eagerly written for, edited, and read by community people. Its theater, weekly topical skits put together by organizers and community people, has a smaller but even more dedicated following. Both are expanding as the level of organization permits. NCUP's neighborhood radio station, transmitting through power lines, is imminent. JOIN also shows movies on organizing and issues, with great effect. These projects have an intrinsic validity—telling the truth. They are easier to set up than economic counter-institutions; and the mainstream proposes a less compelling alternative. . . .

Finally there are *political counter-institutions*, aiming to effect a transfer of legitimacy in more strategic zones. Some, like the Mississippi Freedom Democratic Party, arise because there is simply no other way to accomplish a goal (register voters) ; they can offer alternatives but cannot take power. Others, like the Lowndes County Freedom Party, reject the available alternative of party politics in favor of independent structure. . . .

Some critics, holding fast to the vanishing myth of Southern exceptionalism, would validate such political innovations only for the Black Belt. But in cities where important material needs cannot be achieved for a long time, political counter-institutions might also become serious intermediate objectives. When the good citizens of Los Angeles refuse to pass a bond issue for a hospital in Watts, it makes sense to think about the secession of Watts from Los Angeles. Watts lacks the resources to build a hospital, Los Angeles has them but will not release them. A movement in Watts would have to do some hard thinking to balance the risks of secession against the gains of substantive legitimacy, freedom from the L.A. cops, pressure on would-be allies. Nominal secessions of that sort might light more fires under liberals, churches, and unions than all the more orthodox appeals put together—and make "something of our own" more resistant to melting into other people's crucibles. Yet the movement must continue to see these moves as precedents for deeper changes, not ends in themselves.

Frontal assertions of newly-made legitimacy are probably best adapted to situations of overt, intolerable terror and police tyranny. In cities like Chicago, traditional protest movements—including JOIN's—against police brutality have accomplished no more than the transfer of some of the worst sadists to other ghettos in the city. Riots may temper brutality for a while, get Negroes on the police force, coax liberals to set up *papier-mâché* review boards, but tend to let the cops clamp down all the harder (either directly, as in Watts, or through electoral backlash, as in New York). In the long run the only serious change would have police forces directly accountable to residents, under the law of a community that controls its own resources; but in the present oppressive context this is utopian. To build for that possibility, though, a movement can invent other ways to contain the police, to deprive them of their legitimacy, to erase fear—in the ghetto, and in the city at large. Following the example of a Watts group, JOIN has experimented with a radio-car patrol, run by young neighborhood men, to keep an eye on police behavior. The danger that the counter-structure might become simply a branch of the central structure—local people taking on exactly the old functions—is lessened by self-awareness and constant re-examination. The evidence compiled by the patrol helps undercut the abusive authority of police in the neighborhood—if people can withstand (as often they have not) the new terrorism. At the same time the patrol would tie in with a developing network of lawyers, clergymen, doctors, and liberal people—*itself induced by the publicity of local organizing*—to begin filing damage suits, inhibit some excesses, record some successes, and finally develop a network of informal neighborhood review boards to publicize atrocities and catalyze some political pressures for substantial reforms. Aside from weakening the moral basis of oppressive "law and order," this support promises to open more space (through needed protection) for grass-roots organizing; local people remain in charge but fashion an honest, functional relationship with middle-class allies.

Counter-institutional forms may in fact be the best means to attract middle-class allies for specific purposes, and link them to the ongoing movement. Sometimes direct action itself can spur the initial contacts: Southern demonstrations catalyzed a national grouping of doctors and nurses that has grown into the Medical Committee on Human Rights, which is now committed to more than first-aid; urgent legal needs led to national committees of lawyers and law students with durable ties to local movements. But in both cases it has been the more or less permanently rooted counter-institutional structures that have coaxed *ad hoc* professional actions into more lasting, committed, potentially radical groupings—as allies and direct supports for poor people's groups, and as radical caucuses within the professions. The 1964 Mississippi Freedom Schools probably meant less in the lives of Mississippi children than in their impact on the Northern teachers.

Once these allies are drawn to the movement, they can become functioning radicals with a fresh orientation toward the society as well as toward the meanings and potentials of their professions. Contact with a poor people's movement, more than a merely theoretical grasp of the need to change the relation of professionals to "clients," can prove decisive. First, the professionals can get to know the poor as people, people rooted in a *milieu*, as political actors, not clients; and to fathom, concretely, the consequences of this society for the people at its bottom. Second, they can learn to make their skills accountable to constituencies with collective needs—a new departure for professions that flaunt expertise (e.g., social work) or the law of the marketplace (medicine) where they need not. Third, radical organizers gain access to raise questions about the structure of the profession and its radical requirements. Fourth, as allies are exposed to blatant attempts to repress the movement, they become more open to radical interpretations of the political process. Fifth, they can develop methods of work, within the movement and on its borders, which sustain their political radicalism and give it roots. The more compelling these learning experiences—and the evidence is that they happen, though unevenly—the more likely are professionals to serve as serious defenders of the gains and potentials of grass-roots movements and as self-motivating radicals in their own rights. Against local repressions they can provide "cover"; against national mechanisms of cooptation they can be buffers, helping to protect the integrity of substantive local participation and radical ideas against the onslaughts of centralism and resources. Otherwise, without serious contact, angry "clients" and organized professionals—the two greatest forces for a potent radicalism—are likely to end up racing off as antagonists, hopelessly divided over questions of control and priorities. Much of the burden is on the professionals, to transcend their narrow self-interest and re-discover the professions' essences in an ethic of responsiveness to human need; but community unions should also be looking for ways to encourage the process.

An End to History

by Mario Savio, student in the Department of
Philosophy, Berkeley, and member FSM Steering Committee

Last summer I went to Mississippi to join the struggle there for civil rights. This fall I am engaged in another phase of the same struggle, this time in Berkeley. The two battlefields may seem quite different to some observers, but this is not the case. The same rights are at stake in both places—the right to participate as citizens in democratic society and the right to due process of law. Further, it is a struggle against the same enemy. In Mississippi an autocratic and powerful minority rules, through organized violence, to suppress the vast, virtually powerless majority. In California, the privileged minority manipulates the university bureaucracy to suppress the students' political expression. That "respectable" bureaucracy masks the financial plutocrats; that impersonal bureaucracy is the efficient enemy in a "Brave New World."

In our free-speech fight at the University of California, we have come up against what may emerge as the greatest problem of our nation—depersonalized, unresponsive bureaucracy. We have encountered the organized status quo in Mississippi, but it is the same in Berkeley. Here we find it impossible usually to meet with anyone but secretaries. Beyond that we find functionaries who cannot make policy but can only hide behind the rules. We have discovered total lack of response on the part of the policy makers. To grasp a situation which is truly Kafkaesque, it is necessary to understand the bureaucratic mentality. And we have learned quite a bit about it this fall, more outside the classroom than in.

As bureaucrat, an administrator believes that nothing new happens. He occupies an a-historical point of view. In September, to get the attention of this bureaucracy which had issued arbitrary edicts suppressing student political expression and refused to discuss its action, we held a sit-in on the campus. We sat around a police car and kept it immobilized for over thirty-two hours. At last, the administrative bureaucracy agreed to negotiate. But instead, on the following Monday, we discovered that a committee had been appointed, in accordance with usual regulations, to resolve the dispute. Our attempt to convince any of the administrators that an event had occurred, that something new had happened, failed. They saw this simply as something to be handled by normal university procedures.

The same is true of all bureaucracies. They begin as tools, means to certain legitimate goals, and they end up feeding their own existence. The conception that bureaucrats have is that history has in fact come to an end. No events can occur now that the Second World War is over which can change American society substantially. We proceed by standard procedures as we are.

The most crucial problems facing the United States today are the problem of automation and the problem of racial injustice. Most people who will be put out of jobs by machines will not accept an end to events, this historical plateau, as the point beyond which no change occurs. Negroes will not accept

---

* Reprinted with permission from author.

an end to history here. All of us must refuse to accept history's final judgment that in America there is no place in society for people whose skins are dark. On campus students are not about to accept it as fact that the university has ceased evolving and is in its final state of perfection, that students and faculty are respectively raw material and employees, or that the university is to be autocratically run by unresponsive bureaucrats.

Here is the real contradiction: the bureaucrats hold history as ended. As a result significant parts of the population both on campus and off are dispossessed, and these dispossessed are not about to accept this a-historical point of view. It is out of this that the conflict has occurred with the university bureaucracy and will continue to occur until that bureaucracy becomes responsive or until it is clear the university cannot function.

The things we are asking for in our civil-rights protests have a deceptively quaint ring. We are asking for the due process of law. We are asking for our actions to be judged by committees of our peers. We are asking that regulations ought to be considered as arrived at legitimately only from the consensus of the governed. These phrases are all pretty old, but they are not being taken seriously in America today, nor are they being taken seriously on the Berkeley campus.

I have just come from a meeting with the Dean of Students. She notified us that she was aware of certain violations of university regulations by certain organizations. University friends of Student Non-violent Coordinating Committee, which I represent, was one of these. We tried to draw from her some statement on this great principles, consent of the governed, jury of one's peers, due process. The best she could do was to evade or to present the administration party line. It is very hard to make any contact with the human being who is behind these organizations.

The university is the place where people begin seriously to question the conditions of their existence and raise the issue of whether they can be committed to the society they have been born into. After a long period of apathy during the fifties, students have begun not only to question but, having arrived at answers, to act on those answers. This is part of a growing understanding among many people in America that history has not ended, that a better society is possible, and that it is worth dying for.

This free-speech fight points up a fascinating aspect of contemporary campus life. Students are permitted to talk all they want so long as their speech has no consequences.

One conception of the university, suggested by a classical Christian formulation, is that it be in the world but not of the world. The conception of Clark Kerr by contrast is that the university is part and parcel of this particular stage in the history of American society; it stands to serve the need of American industry; it is a factory that turns out a certain product needed by industry or government. Because speech does often have consequences which might alter this perversion of higher education, the university must put itself in a position of censorship. It can permit two kinds of speech, speech which encourages continuation of the status quo, and speech which advocates changes in it so radical as to be irrelevant in the foreseeable future. Someone may advocate radical change in all aspects of American society, and this I am sure he can do with impunity. But if someone advocates sit-ins to bring about changes in discriminatory hiring practices, this cannot be permitted because it goes against the status quo of which the university is a part. And that is how the fight began here.

The administration of the Berkeley campus has admitted that external, extra-legal groups have pressured the university not to permit students on campus to organize picket lines, not to permit on campus any speech with consequences. And the bureaucracy went along. Speech with consequences, speech in the area of civil rights, speech which some might regard as illegal, must stop.

Many students here at the university, many people in society, are wandering aimlessly about. Strangers in their own lives, there is no place for them. They are people who have not learned to compromise, who for example have come to the university to learn to question, to grow, to learn—all the standard things that sound like clichés because no one takes them seriously. And they find at one point or other that for them to become part of society, to become lawyers, ministers, businessmen, people in government, that very often they must compromise those principles which were most dear to them. They must suppress the most creative impulses that they have; this is a prior condition for being part of the system. The university is well structured, well tooled, to turn out people with all the sharp edges worn off, the well-rounded person. The university is well equipped to produce that sort of person, and this means that the best among the people who enter must for four years wander aimlessly much of the time questioning why they are on campus at all, doubting whether there is any point in what they are doing, and looking toward a very bleak existence afterward in a game in which all of the rules have been made up, which one cannot really amend.

It is a bleak scene, but it is all a lot of us have to look forward to. Society provides no challenge. American society in the standard conception it has of itself is simply no longer exciting. The most exciting things going on in America today are movements to change America. America is becoming ever more the utopia of sterilized, automated contentment. The "futures" and "careers" for which American students now prepare are for the most part intellectual and moral wastelands. This chrome-plated consumers' paradise would have us grow up to be well-behaved children. But an important minority of men and women coming to the front today have shown that they will die rather than be standardized, replaceable and irrelevant.

C. From Protest to Resistance to Liberation.

The various New Left experiments with political action always seem to end by asking one question. For what purpose should action be used? By the end of the decade the purpose had become clear: resistance and liberation. An intolerable war linked to political trials around the country indicated that repressive measures were on the rise. Through its actions, the New Left made clear to the Establishment that the lines of action had indeed been drawn.

Michael Farber makes his NO a political act. At the same time that it constitutes a negation of immoral power, it affirms the capacity of men to resist that power. Resistance becomes an act of political communion with others.

Frank Bardacke and Tom Hayden make a similar appeal in their analysis of the People's Park episode. The assault on the park and on the area around the campus is seen as an attempt to destroy the radical community in Berkeley. The community was able to resist and defend itself because underscoring its foundation is a decade of struggle and organization.

Resistance, in part, is a strategy of defense. Thus Bardacke and Hayden look beyond it toward liberation. They envision increased organization and confrontation, leading to a struggle that will spark a real movement towards liberation in America. In that vision the New Left ends the decade asking not to be included in the old America but to supplant it with a more real kind of equality.

Free Berkeley*

By Frank Bardacke and Tom Hayden

Berkeley is a zone of confrontation, a kind of "front" in the worldwide battle against American capitalism. The fortunes of mighty men—Clark Kerr, Charles Hitch, Ronald Reagan— and the fortunes of mighty institutions—the University, agribusiness, the defense and aerospace industries—are committed in the battle over Berkeley.

Our own fortunes, and those of the movement, also depend on whether Berkeley continues to be a fighting community, an example of rebellion to others.

---

* Reprinted with permission from *The Berkeley Barb*, 22 August 1969.

After a decade of struggle, we have a deeper sense of the place Berkeley. It is not just a place we pass through, enjoying the city's charms in a first flirtatious affair. It is a place to stay, to live, to struggle. We are learning how local struggle can take on international significance.

The importance of our example can be seen in a catalog of past movement events:

● the HUAC demonstrations in 1960 established the right to organize a student movement without bending to the anti-communist paranoia of the 'fifties.

● the Free Speech Movement ignited a nationwide struggle against the odious university machine.

● the Vietnam Day Committee initiated the militant, mass-based anti-war movement calling for immediate withdrawal.

● the Scheer campaign indicated that anti-war sentiment was so strong that it would affect even conventional electoral politics.

● Stop the Draft Week, loosely coordinated with the 1967 Pentagon demonstration, began the phase of fighting in the streets, or, in the rhetoric of the time, moved us "from dissent to resistance."

● the Telegraph Avenue confrontations of summer 1968 created a revolutionary identity for the Street Left and first raised the demand for self-determination in our own turf.

● The People's Park battle began the politics of liberation. We ripped off the Man's land attempting to meet our own needs by creating and trying to defend a space of our own.

● while our radicalism owes a vital amount to the pace-setting example of the black movement, we in turn have been of some value to black revolutionaries like the Panthers. We made it possible for them to work with and take a "class" line towards a white movement, because we were strong enough to support the "Free Huey" demand, Eldridge's presidential campaign and his 139X course.

● the internal problems of our movement have caused our own "revolution within the revolution," resulting in the growth of women's liberation groups and new, more humane and communal attempts at organization.

Certainly this Berkeley stronghold has been crucial to the movement. A large number of radicals in one place, with a common tradition, able to intensify and extend the struggle in their own area, helps to speed up the revolutionary movement everywhere.

Our strengths have made us hateful to bourgeois society. The local conservative forces have had it. While the Gazette calls for the use of an "iron fist" to crush us, family after family is departing Berkeley, taxes are spiralling largely because of greater police expenditures, and commercial and city insurance is impossible to obtain.

The frustrated University is losing its liberal mask: even conventional front-men (in committees on ethnic studies, Chicano affairs, architecture and development) are leaving in protest, while the University proceeds to disqualify its ASUC president, override student sentiment, and expel "hardcore" elements.

The University Police Department seems to have taken over Sproul Hall, and is expanding both its numbers and its search-and-destroy missions in "radical-infested" areas.

We are a National Menace Before the McClellan Committee. Reagan's legal aide described the threat this way:

There is substantial reason to believe that the rampant current philosophy of student revolt has been developed, tested and subcontracted to other institutions throughout the country.

There you have it. In the worried calculations of the ruling class, Berkeley occupies the same key subversive role in the international youth rebellion that, say, Peking does in the Third World liberation movements.

This explains the qualitative change in repression towards us over the past year. The days of "repressive tolerance" when "brutality" was located in Mississippi, or Oakland, are disappearing quickly. Reagan's acceptance of Mario Savio's rhetoric about bureaucratic "knowledge factories" came five years too late to coopt anyone, and Reagan surely knows it.

The shift from the tactics of repressive tolerance to those of fascism was clearest in the Park controversy. Surely, in another town, an institution as wealthy as the University could have worked out a "compromise," or even given away a $1.3 million dollar piece of property. But our action was revolutionary (beyond tolerance) because it happened in Berkeley where the movement has reached threatening dimensions. Our power, example, and our existence as a radical community would only grow larger if we defeated the University's "removal" policy and controlled some land in the strategic South Campus area.

At the highest levels of power. They have made the decision to destroy our community. Some statistics of confrontation since summer 1968 show what we have gone through:

- 22 days of street fighting during six confrontations.
- more than 2,000 arrests.
- over 150 suspensions and expulsions from the University.
- over 40 days of occupation by "mutual-aid" forces from other cities.
- 22 days of National Guard occupation during two crises.
- at least 20 days of local curfew.
- nearly four months of locally-declared "state of disaster" conditions, and nearly five months of state-declared "state of emergency" conditions. There has not been a "normal" period of civilian government in Berkeley this year.
- and, of course, James Rector, and a few less-publicized blacks and hippies, killed by the pigs; artist Alan Blanchard blinded, and about 150 people shot.

Berkeley has been turned into an experimental laboratory for testing repressive techniques: since counter-insurgency has failed, and the use of shotguns, chemical war and aerial coordination has begun, we are quite literally risking our lives to go out in the street. Anyone who thinks it is still a groove to live in Berkeley, or that Berkeley is a nice community with integrated schools, is out of touch with reality. Not our right to smoke dope but our right to survival itself, is at stake in this town from now on.

II

Ten years of struggle have revealed serious weaknesses in our community. Given the present attitudes of the rulers, these weaknesses are now becoming suicidal, as is our reluctance to face them and criticize ourselves.

Weakness number one: We are not really organized for survival. We have struggled together in crisis after crisis, throwing up ad hoc committee after ad hoc committee. But we have been unable to build any mass-based, democratically-run revolutionary organization; and we also have been unable to work together, educate each other, and prepare for struggle between crises.

This disrespect and suspicion toward organization is healthy when we are faced with traditional Leninist parties or "new" parties with old content (like Peace and Freedom). Our emphasis on work, direct action and revolution-from-below has been a great—perhaps our greatest—strength.

But distrust of organization can be elevated into an indulgent and purist philosophy. Our lack of organization makes us prey to opportunism and dilletantism during times of crisis. The tendency of past leaders to vault into leadership during every new crisis stems not from their elitism but from the existing leadership vacuum that Berkeley-style anarchism creates. This pattern also produces in us an attitude of spasmodic protest, lacking any connection to a long-term dedication to commit our lives to the destruction of the system.

"To be organized" does not have to mean a mass organization that inflates bureaucracy while atomizing individuals, nor a highly-disciplined party that acts "for" the party, nor any of the thousand bum structures we have experienced. To be organized means to struggle and prepare for more struggle through whatever machinery proves useful. At its simplest in Berkeley organization means being involved with a group that does political work, develops the thinking and ability of its members, and provides an atmosphere of mutual trust. Berkeley contains little of this except during crisis periods. We are not suggesting that organization substitute for spontaneity. No revolution is simply "organized." Revolutions grow through spontaneous outbreaks in which the imagination and energy of the people often are far ahead of their organized "vanguards." Throughout our own history, spontaneous acts have been crucial. For example, surrounding the police car in FSM, building the barricades in STDW. The source of our strength in the streets has always been spontaneous. But organization—before, during, and after crises —builds the consciousness, spreads the skills, and forges the links that underlie each new upsurge of spontaneous actions.

We will go into the next confrontation with greater experience, but no greater organizational strength, than before. When they drive us off Telegraph, we will have no capacity to boycott stores and landlords, and no capacity to defend ourselves. On the other hand, the pigs will have studied their past mistakes, developed new weapons, increased their forces, and prepared well for the occasion.

But organization is not only needed for arguing politics and preparing for confrontation. We also need organization to demonstrate that we can create alternative ways to meet our needs. We should be creating community institutions like schools, nurseries, day care centers, and our own co-operative stores. Such places give people experience in determining their own lives, and establish a community way of life worth defending. Not to build institutions like these implies defeatism. It means we have to hustle the existing institutions for our survival instead of building new ones through trial and error, which will provide for our needs now and in the future. The lack of such institutions in Berkeley is one of our greatest weaknesses, for it suggests that our radicalism is abstract and temporary rather than concrete and lifelong.

Weakness number two: we are isolated from the community. We have been a white middle-class movement which relates to other insurgent or potentially insurgent people at our leisure. Time after time we have been isolated and alone, and this has enabled propagandists of the ruling class to turn potential friends against us. In the past year there has been a new effort to end this isolation, but it has not gone far enough: students must really feel that they cannot change the schools without a mass popular movement; and community people must see that their vital interests are affected by entrance standards, tracking, research on weapons, new agricultural techniques, and all the instruments of exploitation developed and used by the University.

We must convince the majority of people that Berkeley radicals are not their enemies, and in fact are their friends. We have to be present on the strike picket lines, for example, if we expect working people to begin to see the relevance of our problems to theirs. Instead we are starting to resemble certain student movements in other countries where crippling student strikes go on and on without ever sparking a mass movement in the community or the countryside.

Unfortunately, we deserve to be isolated. We have consistently been unable to work even on Third World problems right here in Berkeley. Many of us were quick to dismiss the TWLF strike because of the mistakes of its leadership, but when was there a Berkeley action where the leaders did not make mistakes? The creation of the People's Pad without consulting the black community was an accurate caricature of our self-centered politics.

We have not even linked up with other white middle class movements very often. The most glaring example is Berkeley High School, where there are large numbers of radical young white people. Over the years many of these students have trekked from their high schools to Sproul or Telegraph to merge into our widely-publicized movements.

As a result of being overshadowed, Berkeley High students have never had an independent movement of their own. Such a movement would broaden our base in Berkeley without causing the usual cutback in radicalism which alliances require.

But perhaps the most serious example of our self-centered politics is our desertion of the Vietnamese. We act as if we "did our anti-war thing" a few years ago. No one denies that mass anti-war mobilizations lost their significance two years ago, and no one denies that our liberation struggle here is severely raising the costs for the US in Vietnam. But our resistance to the war could have been systematic, continuous, and more disruptive, built around issues just as vital to ourselves as they are to the Vietnamese. We could have continued and deepened our attempts to destroy the war machine—from the Oakland Induction Center to campus ROTC to the development by individual social scientists of anti-communist ideology. The explanation for our drifting away from the Vietnam issue, after preparing a huge base of anti-war sentiment, can only be found in our white middle class Berkeley chauvinism. We did not have Vietnam inside our lives.

Weakness number three: We have not been militant enough. The Berkeley movement has advanced largely through a series of political confrontations. In confrontation we learn about our true situation. In ordinary times, rulers can put on a smiling tolerant face, disguise their responsibility for injustice, and hide the reality of armed force which protects their power. More seriously, in ordinary times the people's imagination is crippled by everyday life—a life which appears impossible to change. But when the rulers are challenged by collective struggle the situation is reversed. The enemy is exposed and our imaginations are freed. We begin to see that this social order is not inevitable, we live—however briefly—an alternative life, and we sense the vulnerability of our rulers.

Unfortunately, the Berkeley movement has developed an all too conservative pattern of confrontation. After a militant but peaceful mass action has been attacked by the police, there are one or two days of spontaneous street fighting.

The term "fighting" is too strong, since most of the time is spent in a running death-dance with the pigs. Eventually, we freeze before the power of the State and return to non-disruptive, even friendly, protest. This retreat from confrontation, the desire to stop pushing and probing the limits of the social structure, has many understandable causes.

Take, for example, the Memorial Day March around the fence. A mass meeting called for militance: "Let's rip down the fence May 30." But this insurrectionary act by its very nature but with very real obstacles to getting the action together: the problems of how to structure a march so that it is "legal" enough to get moving without channeling it away from confrontation. problems of how to structure a march so that it is "legal" enough to get moving without channeling it away from confrontation. If the May 30 demand had remained "tear down the fence," large numbers of people still would have come for the action, but the police would easily have blocked the routes and returned us (at best) to spontaneous street fighting. As it turned out, we had the largest march in Berkeley's history, but had to walk helplessly past the Fence, controlled by the rules of our own symbolic politics.

We move away from confrontation because in a crisis we see the choices as either spontaneous street action or structured symbolic marches. This choice must be transcended. The spontaneous actions will not become more militant and sophisticated by some "natural" law of development; but the police tactics certainly will. On the other hand, the structured mass march begins to prove only our mass impotence in the face of a superior force. Within this framework of choice, the police know how to deal with all our tactical options.

In the midst of a crisis, our goal should always be to apply as much force as possible in an attempt to destroy the social order. The cycle of confrontation is not automatic; nor can we turn it on and off as we wish. Confrontation can become caught at a certain level of development. Beyond that level it can no longer develop spontaneously: it must become an art. If we do not recognize confrontation as an art, and consciously develop it towards higher levels, a sense of futility and cynicism can develop towards further confrontations, and begin to rot our community.

We do not have any magic formula for prolonging and extending these confrontations. All we say is that it is necessary to do so, and that it is impossible for our large, loose ad hoc committees to keep up the pressure, then some other form of organization must be developed. Perhaps when we feel ourselves tiring and the pressure easing, it is then time to act in small groups, organizing small provocative actions, holding meetings, intensifying leafletting, in an attempt to push our rulers further up against the wall. In short, we will become more militant only by gaining a sense of organization for self-defense.

the system. In some sense, Rosa Luxembourg's grim aphorism the struggle, the next confrontation will lead to the downfall of We do not suffer from the illusion that if we only keep up is correct: "In revolutionary struggle you lose every battle but the last one." But it is only correct if we understand "lose" to mean fail to take power. In a revolutionary struggle, and in our own confrontations, we always win a great deal. Small, useful concessions result from conflict, like the Sproul microphone and the CPE, and these concessions can only be kept through more struggle.

But, more important than concessions, we build our movement by revealing and therefore demoralizing our rulers, by discovering our unlimited energy and skills, by testing our own strength, and by changing more lives. And we must not delay confrontation for that far off "ripe" moment when we will be "ready." It is always time to intensify the struggle.

These three weaknesses—our failure to organize, our isolation, and our lack of militance—are all rooted in our bourgeois life styles. We shirk back from militant action because we are still attracted to the amenities of middle class American life. In short, we do not yet really believe that our survival depends on the destruction of Capitalism—at crucial moments we think, "Oh, what the hell, I can get by with things as they are." We are isolated because we suffer from that typical bourgeois belief that we are at the center of the Universe, that all others are less imporant and less real. In some ways, we remain spoiled middle class kids. We have failed to organize ourselves because we are highly individualistic, competitive, and unable to trust each other and work together.

We will not solve these problems through T groups or through superhuman efforts to be decent to each other. Bourgeois life styles will disappear only when Capitalism is destroyed. But the struggle to destroy capitalism is a struggle to be born again and, as we fight, we must become new men and women who relate to each other with love and respect.

III

Before we can deal with these problems directly, we must deal with two escapist solutions being advanced by some brothers and sisters: The first comes from certain self-centered "cultural revolutionaries," and the second from certain other-centered "Marxist-Leninists." The first acts us to change our "superstructure," the second our "base." Both positions are revolutionary in tone but dangerously conservative in substance.

"Change your head instead," goes the cultural position, and up to the word "instead" we are in complete agreement. This view starts with one of our generation's greatest insights, that the revolution begins at home, inside our own psyches, when we start being honest about our own situation—who controls us, who we are, who we love, who we hate.

From this approach comes a correct criticism of "the politicos" and their organizations who rhetorically oppose the system by psychologically (or, as Marcuse puts it, "biologically") are thoroughly part of it. The ego rivalries, elitism, materialism, abstract intellectualism, and male chauvinism of the movement are not problems which can be dealt with later. They are problems which can prevent revolution from happening at all, problems which make the Left a kind of psychologically-loyal opposition, hating capitalism abstractly, but unable to reject its social relationships enough to destroy it.

Experiment with drugs, new sexual and human relationships, disregard for the Man's private property, are part of the process of ripping off the bourgeois in ourselves. The leadership of great modern revolutions—in Vietnam, Cuba and China—had to develop a "new morality" and "new man" to survive the hardships of the guerrilla struggle. Although our post-scarcity affluence makes our situation fundamentally different from theirs, we will not overthrow capitalism without becoming a living alternative to its decadence.

But we cannot become "pure" in our heads. The cultural revolution can only begin but never be carried through, without successful struggle against the institutions of the society. The fact is that we have been able to "change our heads" so far not through the magic of drugs—though drugs haven't hurt—but through the struggles we have fought, and especially the struggles that Third World people fight in our behalf.

There is no choice between changing your head and struggling to change your society: one does both at the same time. The Stones owe as much to our movement as we owe to the Stones. Without successful struggle, our cultural revolution will go backwards into a subsidized and commercial form of entertainment. The only culture worth having is a culture that relates to struggle, growing from it and nurturing it in return.

This idea that you should "change your head instead" is linked to a syrupy pacifism. We are told that change will occur when we change their heads by turning them on, giving them good vibes. The power structure, it turns out, is only in our heads, and if ignored, will go away. We will hollow out the psychic foundations until the system peacefully falls. To confront the system in battle is to become "like them": full of hate, ambition, etc. Talk of self-defense, according to this line, simply provokes those who would not attack us if we just were quiet.

During the Park crisis, these ideas were so rampant in Berkeley that some "revolutionaries" were blaming the street fighters for causing the violence. Some organizers of the March were said to be on a "death trip" behaving "just like the pigs," and so forth. These cultural revolutionaries spent most of their time organizing to spread their paranoia everywhere in the crowds, held workshops on how to isolate "agitators," purchased thousands of flowers and gave them to the pigs, and raved afterwards about the march being a "success" because it was nonviolent.

The same tendencies appeared more subtly in our people's attitude towards the National Guard. The realization that Guardsmen are not professional pigs is a step forward in consciousness, and attempts to split or neutralize the Guard occupying Berkeley are crucial. But many people declared that the Guardsmen were "our brothers," and conveniently erased the fact that the Guardsmen were accepting orders to pacify and, if necessary, brutalize us. The degree of fraternization with the Guard surely upset Reagan and the military commanders. But the degree of false fraternization based on fear allowed the Guard to successfully do its job: move us about and clear us away with a minimum of violence.

Let us be clear: we are not implying that the March should have been turned into an insurrection, only that it fell far short of the kind of confrontation which was needed. We should have surrounded the fence (like the Pentagon and Chicago Hilton were confronted), angrily exposing to everyone that only raw outside military force stood between us and our park. That scene coupled with an organized strike of the city and UC might have won our demands, and certainly would have created the mood in which small groups might have ripped the fence down. As it was, the psychological effect favored the military: we were permitted a kind of funeral march to have a last look at our land.

This set of cultural ideas becomes most dangerous when it moves from the idea that "revolution begins with me" to a notion that "the revolution is for me." People believe that the revolution has come because they have managed to hustle a welfare check or whatever, and they do not have to work. They no longer feel for others or for a community of people. They see rebellion and revolution as an individual act, and they dream of a very American individualized independence rather than of collective community freedom. Too many of us are exactly like our "easy rider" brothers, and we are heading towards the same fate.

A second solution being advanced is the new/old theory which says essentially: let us proletarianize ourselves. The argument usually goes like this: Point one, our experience in the student movement has shown us that students can't make the revolution alone. Point two, we have to make alliances with those who have revolutionary potential, the working class.

Or an alternative argument to the same conclusion: One, students are middle class (or from the "intermediate layers" of society). Two, it is the Third World movements, and the white working class who together will make the revolution. We have to support these Third World movements, and work among the white working class. If we work at all around the university or street culture, it should be to put forward "working class politics" rather than student "politics of privilege." We should involve students on campus in actions against imperialism and in favor of working class admissions. As a high priority, we should encourage our people to leave the campus, leave their youth culture, and begin organizing in working class communities.

So much of this can be disastrous. Certainly we remain isolated at our own peril, certainly we cannot make the revolution alone, certainly we must build alliances with other revolutionary movements. But when these arguments are pushed too far, they leave no room for students to struggle as students, no room for hippies to fight for their identity. Campus and street rebellions are no longer called for, and we are told that in order to relate to workers we have to cut our hair, stop smoking pot, deny who we are.

Why did many in SDS, the New Left organization, adopt this distorted proletarianism? Why did some of us forget most of what we learned from experience these past ten years, and nearly all of what makes us a "new" left? In addition to the good reasons, here were some bad ones. The call to proletarianize ourselves is another expression of the white middle class self-hatred which has bedeviled the New Left for so long. We experienced it in the early civil rights movement, in thē SDS community organizing projects in working class and black neighborhoods, and in the present assertion that, as white middle class people, we are not "real."

The self-hatred was coupled with an organizational struggle against Progressive Labor, in which many felt it was necessary to prove that they were just as Marxist (even just as Stalinist!) as PL.

Think of how different SDS ideology would be if it had been invaded by Yippies and White Panthers rather than PL. At least SDS would have had to remain true to its own roots, and would today be more in touch with American youth of all classes.

The major premise of this proletarian argument is simply wrong. Our problems are not only real, they are genuinely revolutionary. We are a post-scarcity generation who cannot relate to competitive capitalism, and who are being severely pressured into accepting managerial or service roles within an Empire which violates every decent value transmitted to us. Not only are we crucial to the success of capitalism objectively, we have continually shown the subjective capacity to formulate and move toward revolutionary goals.

While many of our needs flow from a class privilege that must be abolished, we have demonstrated crucial needs which are shared by nearly all of humanity, needs which only a revolutionary communist society would fulfill. Even at this stage of struggle, the expression of our needs touches a receptive chord in millions of other people, many of them working class people: our music and drug cultures, our hatred of the draft, are only the most obvious examples.

We can achieve certain objectives without waiting for the working class to lead or even join the revolution. We are not weightless people from a vague "intermediate layers," only able to have power when united with the working class. The Marxists in Vietnam and Cuba certainly know this; they repeatedly have welcomed student and anti-war movements as a crucial brake on imperialist escalation. We have disrupted the war effort and could disrupt it even further. And the ruling class knows it. Fortune magazine has devoted an entire issue to the threat on the campuses. Their term for us—"forerunners"—implies exactly that we are growing in numbers and in strategic significance.

The white industrial working class is not the "vanguard" or only agency of revolutionary change. When Marx spoke of the industrial proletariat being "the" agency of change, his conception was that at the time of the revolution the proletariat would make up the most exploited and most numerous group in the population. Today, the white industrial proletariat is a numerical minority, infinitely fragmented and divided in the work places, living on credit with a stake in demanding the protection of their precarious privileges.

Most other Americans are "proletarian" also, in that they have no control of the means of production, but their long-term class interest is submerged in their short-term differences of color, status, income, etc. Those who show the most signs of possible revolutionary needs happen to be the youth of all backgrounds.

Young people are the least settled and accommodated, and tend to have greater aspirations than the older generation. From their vantage point, it is easiest to see that the "opportunities" offered by society—unemployment, the army, high schools and colleges, the trade unions—are rotten compared to America's potential.

Of course the revolution cannot be made without the industrial working class—they have numbers and power in the productive system—but there is no evidence in practice that they are the vanguard force. Advanced capitalism is so deeply rooted, and decaying at such a furious pace at all levels of our society, that people of many different class backgrounds can push the system to its limits by struggling where they are. We should not choose our vanguards in theory. They will identify themselves in action.

We will not build alliances by denying who we are, and it is elitist to assume that workers—unlike blacks—need students to radicalize them. The most successful student-worker alliance in a modern capitalist state (Paris 968 was begun by anarchist students who seized control of buildings and generally defied all of bourgeois society. Their shock actions opened a breach in the suffocating reality of France, and the working class—despite the reactionary ravings of the Communist trade unionists—moved to occupy their factories. It will not happen that way all the time, and we are sure there were many student attitudes which contained prejudice towards the workers (and vice versa). But you do not build alliances by destroying your own movement, or by orienting the organizing of students primarily around the needs of workers.

This does not mean that we should not search for issues on campus relevant both to ourselves and to the needs of the revolutionary struggles of the working class. For example, during the Standard Oil strike we should have made it impossible for Standard Oil to recruit on campus.

Our own tiny experience with white workers in the Bay Area in fact suggests that campus militance attracts young workers rather than alienating them. In an article analyzing the Richmond strike, Bob Avakian, one of our comrades with an extremely "proletarian" view, says:

. . . it was the younger workers who have kept the strike going, with the help of students. Many of these younger workers have long hair, wear beards, mustaches, and sideburns, have spent time around Berkeley, and a few have even participated in anti-war marches and Stop the Draft Week . . . It is these younger workers who have stood up to the police and have twice engaged in pitched battle, clubs in hand, against a company goon squad . . .

Much of this new political emphasis flows from the healthy tendency of veteran radicals to finally leave Berkeley. It is all very well and good for people who have gone through their student rebellions and who no longer want to work with students to go out and become working class organizers. Not only is it all right—it is splendid. But in their effort to overcome Berkeley chauvinism, these people should not call for energy to simply "flow out of Berkeley" (as someone demanded at the SDS regional meeting recently). These people should not tell students and street people to forego as "bourgeois" a struggle with their brothers and sisters for control of their lives.

This is not to say that every generation of students has to duplicate the mistake of FSM, or even the mistakes of People's Park. Clearly, our struggles have helped us to a more sophisticated notion of UC and Berkeley. But students should still be encouraged to destroy the University as a place that produces the managers of advanced capitalism, and to try to create a vision of a University that struggles to teach and learn the skills necessary for all men to win their freedom. And street people should be encouraged to make their boldest visions even bolder, and fight like guerrillas for the survival of their culture.

To channel this boiling energy away from new confrontations and towards building a working-class base, at a time when the Berkeley struggle means so much, may seem very "Marxist," but in reality is a profoundly conservative doctrine, for it tells people to postpone the fight. A revolutionary strategy must combine the needs for Berkeley radicals to intensify the struggle here while building alliances throughout the Bay Area and the state.

IV

And so, What Is To Be Done?

Our position is that before anything can be done, a greater and more serious consciousness of the Berkeley crisis is necessary in our community. Developments of the past ten years have brought us to a new situation. Our survival here as a radical movement can no longer be taken for granted. We have to take more seriously what we have created, overcome our faults, extend and defend Berkeley as a stronghold for the entire movement.

Our strategy should be to continue the polarization until a radical and fully organized majority exists here, until the Gazette readers move out, until we are lined up against only the national power structure and their local lackeys.

In the space we create, we should extend our revolutionary culture and politics as far as our imaginations allow, we should begin to govern our own community as directly as possible, we should create belts of affection and support with other movements everywhere, and we should be able to defend ourselves if worse comes to worst. To be specific on a few points:

1. Our underlying forms of organization should flow from our emerging character as a revolutionary community. Most of us find it best to work in small groups—they extend from radical sects who consider themselves the "vanguard," to the Free Church, to radical caucuses in local unions, to the insurgent sociologists, to the staff of underground media, to the RSU work projects, to the living communes, to the Revolutionary Bakers (we are leaving out several hundred others). We will try in these groups to treat each other as equals; work, struggle, and play together; build human relationships that transcend our bourgeois life styles; and become centers of direct action in the struggle to overthrow capitalism.

2. The essence of being organized is to have a network of functional community institutions to serve our interests. The

Tribe should be supported and transformed even more into a community service. A radical tenants union is needed for a long-overdue rent strike. We must work with small homeowners and shoppers in campaign against taxes and prices, and where possible form co-ops of our own. We need a free medical clinic, but more than that, we need hundreds of medically-trained people. We need ways to take care of abortion needs and drug needs. We need police-observer and self-defense units. We need a revolutionary counter institution chipping away and exposing the University. We need a Liberation School as a training center. We need communes and crash pads. We need a women's liberation center and communes. We need one hell of a legal defense operation. Each of these might be reformist standing alone, but in a real alliance they become the institutional basis of revolution.

We must remember that we will not live in a state of continual confrontation. This network of institutions is necessary to give us sustenance and support in ordinary times, and to provide us with strength during crises. Moreover, it is only through these institutions that we can feel in our daily lives the promise of another life.

3. The major organizational step we suggest is the formation of a Tribal Council or "collective of collectives." This would not be another mass organization composed of isolated individuals and led by a small steering committee. It would be an arena of cross-fertilization between real groups of people with their own projects. It would be a stimulus to creating independent projects, and a forum where people in those projects could work out their relationship to the rest of the community. It would not have power to make decisions for the individual collectives. The Council would be a place where every group would be encouraged to bring their programs and ideas for mutual discussion. The 13-point Liberation Program, a manifesto issued by a group of collectives after the Park crisis, is a good beginning in this direction. It should serve as a focus for the development of a more thorough revolutionary program written by more groups over the coming year.

4. We must immediately extend the movement to all possible revolutionary forces in Berkeley—especially to the high school and black community. We should see the youth—street, student, worker—as the main moving force, but we should unite wherever

possible with the traditional liberal-left community. We should send people to every important action (strikes, conferences, etc.) outside Berkeley to build alliances.

5. Our politics must be international in focus, not simply limited to community issues. We must continue the attack on racism, militarism and the war, and corporate capitalism, especially where University involvement can be impeded. We must continue raising questions that will spread to other movement centers around the country. We must send travellers to Cuba, Vietnam, France, West Germany, Italy, everywhere in the world, to share experiences.

And if we try to do all this, what can we expect? Who knows, but history might look on us in one of two ways.

First, a scenario of defeat:

Berkeley in the 1960s was one of the more militant centers of the new radicalism. But several bloody confrontations with the police and the army climaxed by the killing of several score unarmed people in one week, caused the Berkeley resistance to fragment and break. Sectarianism instilled confusion in political circles, and the so-called "street people" withdrew into mysticism. Harassment on petty charges became too severe for even the most hardened elements, and they withdrew into rural areas or emigrated to Europe. When the campus and installed highrise faculty housing, the famous Telegraph Avenue culture dried up completely. The transfer of University liberal arts programs to Santa Cruz finished the transformation of Berkeley into the nation's major scientific research center.

By the twentieth year since the US invasion of Vietnam, American society was in chaos marked by student riots, wildcat strikes and random acts of disobedience between individuals everywhere. The unofficial civil war in California, which eventually spread throughout the US, seemed to have its tangled roots in the Bay Area. Acting in response to a successful Black Panther raid on Oakland police headquarters, the students at Berkeley High School began a strike which eventually spread to the long-troubled University of California. By the sixth month of the Berkeley strike, Eshelman Hall was the barricaded headquarters of the Berkeley Liberation Front (BLF) which seemed at times to hold endless meetings in all corners of the mammoth building. After three months of negotiations ended in bitter failure, most of the faculty accepted teaching positions elsewhere and many moved away from Berkeley altogether. Telegraph Avenue was largely in ruins due to repeated fires, and it resembled a strange Casbah of hippie traders who were reportedly connected to a military underground. Blacks in cooperation with supermarket workers seized all the supermarket produce and distributed it in their communities.

Several country communes delivered further foodstuffs and this combined with truckloads of food delivered secretly from a friendly Teamsters caucus provided enough food for everyone. Although affinity groups and female communes had gone underground after repeated police terror, thousands of hippie squatters freely occupied deserted mansions and homes in the hills. Working class families from the nearby "revolutionary union movement" settled in liberated housing. No City records of property ownership were any longer available after BLF agents staged a suicidal attack on the old City Hall. The absence of rent was a welcome relief for those workers who had been laid off during the previous year's sweeping strikes. The Alameda Labor Council tried to prevent the local workers from getting goods into Berkeley, and ordered everyone to resume work while they negotiated for higher wages. The workers still occupying factories rejected negotiations and continued producing goods to help Berkeley survive. Armed forces under direct federal control were stationed in the North Oakland Hills. Except for aerial reconnaissance, they remained at a distance from the Telegraph area after the burning of their original headquarters in Sproul Hall and the complete destruction by blacks of their second headquarters in the North Oakland flatlands. Infiltrated BLF agents apparently played a role in upsetting military morale and planning. But the major break in Army morale occurred when a captain tried to lead a reconnaissance mission deep behind Berkeley's city limits. Once the soldiers were safely separated from the main body of armed forces, they shot the captain and joined the BLF. Their broadcasts over liberated KPFA to other soldiers was judged to be largely responsible for the phenomenal desertion rate among the occupying forces. Two of the most daring deserters brought with them a kidnaped general and two key intelligence officers. This spectacular operation seemed to accelerate the disintegration of the armed forces, and provide a short-term deterrent for the revolutionaries against bombing or long-range shelling. As the system of controls continued to crumble, rioting became commonplace in Los Angeles and other major cities, and the official closing of the state educational system apparently freed young people to go directly into the resistance. Although the government attempted nationwide news control, the existence of a nationwide revolutionary network, and especially the courage of young "newsreel" photographers spread the message to other areas where strikes were also gathering strength. The beginning of the end for the American ruling class, called the "babylonians" by the rebels, came with the coordinated rising against several hundred police stations followed by insurrections throughout the cities of California.

A fantasy concocted from the crazed Berkeley atmosphere? Well, with the French students we say: our fantasies come from experience and we will fight until our fantasies become reality.

A Time to Say No

Michael Ferber

[During the first "antidraft" day held on October 16, 1967, 1,158 young men sent their draft cards to the federal authorities in 18 cities. This act of civil disobedience, punishable by a maximum of $10,000 fine and five years in prison, signified the refusal to cooperate in any manner whatever with the Selective Service System. Michael Ferber, a draft resister on the basis of religious conviction, was tried together with Doctor Benjamin Spock and three other men accused of illegally counselling virtually all American draft-age males to refuse military service. The following is the text of a speech given by Michael Ferber in the Arlington Street Church of Boston and published in *Resistance*, June 15, 1968.]

We are gathered in this church today in order to do something very simple: to say No. We have come from many different places and backgrounds and we have many different ideas about ourselves and the world, but we have come here to show that we are united to do one thing: to say No. Each of our acts of returning our draft cards is our personal No; when we put them in a single container or set fire to them from a single candle we express the simple basis of our unity.

But what I wish to speak about now is what goes beyond our saying No, for no matter how loudly we all say it, no matter what ceremony we perform around our saying it, we will not become a community among ourselves nor effective agents for changing our country if a negative is all we share. Albert Camus said that the rebel, who says no, is also one who says Yes, and that when he draws a line beyond which he will refuse to cooperate he is affirming the values on the other side of that line. For us who come here today, what is it that we affirm, what is it to which we can say Yes?

To be honest we have to admit that we in the Resistance still disagree about a great many things, whether we speak out about them or not. For example, here we all are in a church, and yet for some of us it is the first time we've been inside one for years. Here we are receiving the help of many clergymen, and yet some of us feel nothing but contempt for the organized religions that they represent. Some of us, therefore, feel a certain hypocrisy in being part of this service.

But it would not surprise me if many of the clergymen who are here today feel some of the same contempt for organized religion that our unreligious or anti-religious brothers feel. They know better than we do the long and bloody history of evils committed in the name of religion, the long history of compromise and Erastian subservience to political power, the long history of theological hair-splitting and the burning of heretics, and they feel more deeply than we do the hypocrisy of Sunday (or Saturday) morning. Perhaps the things that made some of us leave the church are the very things that made some of them become ministers, priests, and rabbis, the very things that bring them here today. Many of them will anger their superiors or their congregations by being here but they are here anyway.

There is a great tradition within the church and synagogue

which has always struggled against the conservative and worldly forces that have always been in control. It is a radical tradition, a tradition of urgent impulses to go to the root of the religious dimension of human life. This tradition in modern times has tried to recall us to the best ways of living our lives: the way of love and compassion, the way of justice and respect, the way of facing other people as human beings and not as abstract representatives of something alien and evil. It tries to recall us to the reality behind religious ceremony and symbolism, and it will change the ceremony and symbolism when the reality changes.

As a part of this service we will break bread together. We do this, however, not because some churches happen to take Communion; we do this for one of the root reasons for Communion itself: that men around the world and for all time have found it good to eat together when they are sharing in something important.

The radical tradition is still alive: it is present here in this church. Those of us who disregard organized religion, I think, are making a mistake if they also disregard this tradition and its presence today. This tradition is something to which we can say Yes.

There is another disagreement among us, or if not a disagreement then a difference in attitude toward what we are doing today. It is a difference that cuts through the other differences, perhaps because it is a little inside each of us, and it leads to a mistake that we are liable to make no matter how else we agree or differ. In religious terms, it is to dwell too much on the possibility of the Apocalypse; in political terms, it is to dwell too much on the possibility of a Utopian Society. We must not confuse the ceremony and symbolism of today's service with the reality that we are only a few hundred people with very little power. And we must not confuse the change inside each of us, important though that may be, with the change that we have yet to bring about in this country and the world. Neither the Revelation nor the Revolution is at hand, and to base our hopes and plans on them would be a tragic blunder.

Maybe all of us—Leftists or Liberals, Reformers or Revolutionaries, Radical Religionists or Hippies—maybe all of us are apocalyptarians, I don't know. Surely something else besides a cold rational calculation of sociological options has brought us here to this church. And surely we are in this church partly to celebrate the occasion of our noncooperation (and many of us will celebrate in a somewhat different way at parties with friends tonight). But let us not be deceived. The sun will rise tomorrow as it does every day, and when we get out of bed the world will be in pretty much the same mess it is in today. American bombers will continue to drop incendiary bombs on the Vietnamese people and American soldiers will continue to "pacify" the villages. The ghettos will continue to be rotten places to live in. Black and Mexican farm workers will continue to get miserable wages. America's schools will continue to cripple the minds and hearts of its pupils. And the American Selective Service System will continue to send young men out to the slaughter.

Today is not the End. Today is the Beginning.

This is the Beginning because, very simply, we have to dig in for the long haul. It is not going to be easy to change this country. To change it is going to mean struggles and anguish day in and day out for years. It will mean incredible efforts at great human cost to gain a few inches of ground. It will mean people dedicating their lives and possibly losing them for a cause we can only partly define and whose outcome we can only guess at. We must say Yes to the long struggle ahead or this service will be a mockery.

To some extent this argument depends on terminology rather than fact. Today we have heard our situation described in religious terms, moral terms, political terms, legal terms, and psychological terms. Very few of us are at home in all these different modes of speech, and each of us habitually uses only one of them to talk and think in. But what is happening today should make it clear that these different modes of speech all overlap one another and they often all say the same essential things. Albert Camus, who struggled in a more serious Resistance than ours, believed that politics is an extension of morality, that the truly moral man is engaged in politics as a natural outcome of his beliefs.

To return to Nick's concern, the real difference is not between the moral man and the political man, but between the mon whose moral thinking leads him to political action and the man whose moral thinking leads him no farther than to his own "sinlessness." It is the difference between the man who is willing to dirty himself in the outside world and the man who wishes to stay "clean" and "pure."

Now this kind of "sinlessness" and "purity" is arrogant pride, and I think we must say No to it. The martyr who offers himself meekly as a lamb to the altar is a fool unless he has fully taken into account the consequences of his sacrifice not only to himself but to the rest of the world. We cannot honor him for his stigmata or his purple hearts unless he has helped the rest of us while he got them.

So then what are we to do? We must look at ourselves once more. We all have an impulse to purification and martyrdom and we should not be ashamed of it. But let us be certain that we have thought through the consequences of our action in the outside world, and that these consequences are what we want to bring about. Let us make sure we are ready to work hard and long with each other in the months to come, working to make it difficult and politically dangerous for the government to prosecute us, working to help anyone and everyone to find ways of avoiding the draft, to help disrupt the working of the draft and the armed forces until the war is over. Let us make sure we can form a community. Let us make sure we can let others depend on us.

If we can say Yes to these things, and to the religious tradition that stands with us today, and to the fact that today marks not the End but a Beginning, and to the long hard dirty job ahead of us—if we can say Yes to all this, then let us come forward together to say No to the United States government.

Then let our Yes be the loudest No our government ever heard.

NACLA: Who Rules Columbia?

[The clamorous occupation of Columbia University in New York was based on the struggle against a university directed by a nonacademic administration which represented the connections between "research and education, on the on hand, and the military-industrial interests of high finance, on the other.

"Who Rules Columbia?" prepared by NACLA, is an analytical documentation on the extra-academic interests which control the university and determine its orientation and programs. Selections from the document are reprinted below. NACLA pamphlet, 1968.]

Introduction

There has been a failure to understand the real issues behind the Columbia uprising. The press has put forth a variety of misleading theories to explain the rebellion: the generation gap, the plotted leftist putsch, the failure of the university to respond to current and changing student needs, breakdown in communication, impatience, a sort of Rite of Spring, general anxiety over the Vietnam war . . . theories which obfuscated the truth.

This pamphlet has been produced to clarify and explain the central issues. It will attempt to show concretely how Columbia University is set up not to service the needs of its own constituency—faculty and students—but rather to service outside interests which, by controlling Columbia finances, effectively control its policy. These outside interests, represented on the Board of Trustees, have organized the university as a "factory" designed to produce the skilled technicians and management personnel which the U.S. industrial and defense apparatus needs. The millions channeled into the university coffers by the agents of these interests are, for them, essentially an investment in people which, like any investment, is expected to yield certain returns.

The concept of the university as an investment determines the nature of grading systems and scholarship mechanisms which provide the rewards and punishments that channel human talents into specified occupations. The examination system does not test learning as such. Creativity and originality are sacrificed; testing is geared to show the ability to perform under the pressure and to function in an hierarchy which channels instructions from the top down.

Our analysis focuses upon two sources outside the university from which Columbia trustees and key administrators derive their power: 1) the control of money (we will show how Columbia's dependence on outside sources of income affects it internal policy) ; and 2) the control of strategic decision-making positions maintained by their corporate, defense and foundation connections (we will examine the organizational associations of the trustees to show that the interests they represent are those which the university curriculum and finances are manipulated to serve).

This control by non-indigenous and non-academic interests is the crucial issue behind the student rebellion. The student contention that the trustees represent illegitimate power is based on a concept fundamental to democracy: that the authority of the rulers is legitimate only insofar as it represents the ruled. By seizing the university buildings, the students sought to dramatize the illegitimacy of the authority of the trustees and to effect, if only briefly, a redistribution of power. The student action shattered two fundamental aspects of control: property was seized, violating one of the most sacred of ideas; and, with the exposure of Kirk's files, the veil of secrecy was torn away (secrecy has always been one of the strongest weapons of control).

However, we have derived our analysis from open sources: *Standard & Poor's Directory, Who's Who in America, The New York Times,* financial magazines and corporation prospectuses. We assumed that major power decisions were made at board meetings and that from an analysis of the interests represented therein, we could predict what would happen in a given situation. The documents liberated from Grayson Kirk's office clearly substantiate our theories. They are in fact the proto-textbook which negates everything the students were being taught at Columbia; the courses were irrelevant or themselves a form of pacification; what they taught was abstract, misleading, calculated to conceal the roles for which students were being trained.

International Corporations: Administering the Empire

After World War II heavy surplus profits from consolidated industries and the saturation of home markets created a need for either heavy investments domestically (which would have to be financed through a radical restructuring of the capitalist organization of the economy) or heavy investment expansion abroad. The larger corporations chose to extend their foreign frontiers and today we find such giants as Standard Oil (N.J.), Texaco,

Colgate-Palmolive, Singer and National Cash Register deriving over half their profits from foreign sales. Direct investments (outright U.S. holdings in plants and equipment) have sky-rocketed from $5 billion to $55 billion between 1945 and the present. Between 1960 and 1965 alone nearly 2,200 companies engaged in about 6,000 separate activities—primarily construction of new plants and the expansion of existing operations.

As the corporations have extended their overseas operations they have required greatly increased numbers of men to manage their investments: men trained in international law, international business management, diplomacy, languages, public relations and social scientists who are experts in foreign cultures. The corporate financial interests turned to the university to fulfill these needs, offering generous amounts of money, privileges for university administrators and high-level access to the prestigious, exciting world of international affairs in return. Columbia's School of International Affairs was created in 1945 to fulfill these needs.

As indicated on the "Top 22" chart, seven of Columbia's rulers have primary ties to either U.S. corporations or non-profit organizations with an international domain. Grayson Kirk was the first director to join Mobil Oil's board from outside its corporate ranks (in 1950). Mobil Oil is heavily dependent on foreign reserves in North Africa and the Near East for it survival. Frederick Kappel is a director of Standard Oil Company which derives over half its profits from foreign sales. William Burden's American Metals Climax has extensive mining interests in Southern Africa.

Several of the "Top 22" occupy prominent positions in the cultural penetration winning converts to the American way which facilitates corporate expansion abroad. Kirk and Lawrence Wien are both trustees of the Institute of International Education which handles all U.S. Student exchanges and channels foreign students to meet the needs of U.S. business abroad. Other trustees and administrators play key roles in organizations financing foreign cultural and intellectual programs such as the Asia Foundation, African-American Institute, America-Korea Foundation and the Near East Foundation.

Since the most enlightened elements in the corporate and financial elite (among others) wish to avoid as much as possible the tensions and dislocations caused by war and direct confrontation, they backed the creation of a diplomatic and intelligence apparatus for channeling and manipulating events to make conflict less disruptive. President Kirk's previous contact with the international diplomatic and intelligence community through his academic posts in international affairs and the State Department's security section facilitated Columbia's training of diplomats and intelligence personnel at the School of International Affairs. The role of Columbia administrators and trustees in such foreign policy-making and intelligence organizations as the Council on Foreign Relations, Asia Foundation and CIA are discussed below.

Columbia University also trains specialized technicians and produces some of the new technology needed by these international corporations. For example, the booming offshore oil industry benefits directly from the technology developed at Columbia's Lamont Geological Observatory.

With the recent increase in foreign investments in the Third World and the increased threat (more and more overshadowing the previous "threat" of Soviet communism) of Third World nationalism, U.S. corporate and financial interests have stressed nation-building in the poor countries. By nation-building they mean creating a favorable infrastructure for capital investment. This involves, among other things, penetration and manipulation of those more "primitive" and esoteric societies and co-opting indigenous elites, and requires anthropologists, sociologists, linguists, political theorists, journalists and psychologists familiar with these societies. The SIA accommodated these needs by adding institutes in Third World studies.

The School of International Affairs

The School of International Affairs (SIA) has become, in the space of a few years, one of Columbia's largest and most important divisions. When founded in 1946, the School operated on a total budget of $60,000; by 1964 the School's annual budget was well over a million dollars, and the Regional Institutes each accounted for hundreds of thousands of dollars more. In 1967, the School listed a Faculty and staff of over 150 members, which included some of the most prestigious—and powerful—figures in the Columbia community. President Grayson Kirk and Vice-President Truman both hold academic positions on the SIA's Faculty.

Originally composed of the School itself and the Russian Institute, the SIA's empire now encompasses eight Regional Institutes (each representing a major segment of the world), and several dozen research projects and institutes. In 1964, the School launched a $32-million fund-raising campaign to expand its activities further, and to finance a new building for the School. The building, named the Edward John Noble Building after the School's heaviest contributor, is now under construction at 118th Street and Amsterdam Ave., on a site once occupied by apartments.

The purpose of the SIA has never been in doubt: to train experts in international affairs and foreign areas for administrative positions in America's expanding overseas empire. This function is set forth clearly in a description of the School which appears in the Columbia University *Bulletin*: "The School of International Affairs is a professional school which was established in 1946 with the purpose of training, in conjunction with the regional institutes, a select group of students for staff and administrative programs in international fields." That this task is being realized can be shown by statistics on the activities of SIA alumni: in 1967, Dean Andrew Cordier estimated that 40 percent of the School's graduates worked in the international agencies of the U.S. Government, while another large segment worked for corporations, foundations or law firms in international activities.

Columbia and the U.S. Intelligence Community

The very nature of the Cold War struggle against Communism and the drive for empire require extensive non-military resources. The U.S. intelligence community, under the direction of the Central Intelligence Agency, is in charge of enlisting the expertise and the cover of non-governmental organizations. Through covert penetration of civilian branches of the government, voluntary groups, corporations, law firms, research centers, cultural projects, foundations and universities, the CIA is able to mobilize and coordinate for government service much of the seemingly a-political work of U.S. civilian society.

The primary tasks of the U.S. intelligence community are gathering and analyzing strategic information for decision-makers and positioning trained personnel in key locations to manipulate the course of events. (For a history and discussion of the CIA see, Wise and Ross, *The Invisible Government*.) Like several large universities, Columbia offers excellent opportunities for achieving these goals. Most of the evidence points to indirect relationships, but because the CIA is closed and secret and because the Columbia Administration refuses to discuss its CIA relations, it is quite possible that CIA-CU ties are far more direct and pervasive than the public data now indicates. In fact, our own information indicates that these ties are so direct as to involve a highly influential group of men in dual positions of leadership—inside Columbia *and* in the CIA itself.

One level of association involves individuals connected with Columbia who are also affiliated with CIA-related organizations. Three types of CIA-relationships are identified in the following table.

CIA-Related Organizations

I. ORGANIZATIONS HEAVILY FUNDED BY CIA:
   Asia Foundation
   African-American Institute
   American Society of African Culture
   Committee of Correspondence
   Free Europe Committee

II. ORGANIZATIONS WHICH RECEIVED SOME FUNDS FROM THE CIA:
   Institute for Int'l Education
   John H. Whitney Trust
   American Council for Emigrés in the Professions

III. COVERTLY PASSED CIA FUNDS:
   Fairfield Foundation
   Foundation for Youth and Student Affairs
   Cleveland H. Dodge Foundation
   Edward John Noble Foundation

David, Josephine and Winfield Baird Foundation, Inc.
William Benton Foundation
Catherwood Foundation
W. Alton Jones Foundation
J. M. Kaplan Fund, Inc.
Lucius N. Littauer Foundation
Aaron E. Norman Fund, Inc.
Rubicon Foundation

The Defense-Research Nexus

The military plays two roles during the period of empire expansion and consolidation. Since access to foreign markets through trade and investment is essential, the military maintains the trade routes, first with the Navy and now with the Air Force. Secondly, conspicuous U.S. military presence and periodic demonstrations of force serve to dampen the development of national resistance to U.S. penetration.

There has been a shift in U.S. military strategy from massive retaliation to the use of limited war as the Soviet "threat" has declined and the "threat" of third world nationalism has increased. As nationalists increasingly engage in guerilla warfare [as in Vietnam and Guatemala] the Defense Department is forced to rely on sophisticated technology to readjust the balance of power. It is the role of the University to provide vital technological weaponry.

Columbia's "Top 22" include good examples of the defense complex. William Burden's Lockheed Aircraft and Moore's General Dynamics together received 10% [$3.6 billion] of all U.S. military contracts. Burden is also Chairman of the Board of the Institute for Defense Analyses which specializes in the evaluation of advanced weaponry and counterinsurgency methods, and serves as the idea factory of the Defense Department. The section below on the Institute for Defense Analyses describes its other close relationships with Columbia. John Dunning, a trustee of Columbia's Riverside Research Institute [RRI], a Defense Department consultant and expert on atomic energy, is a director of three private corporations dependent on military contracts. Dunning's City Investing Corporation, a major subcontractor of Burden's Lockheed Aircraft, manufactures spray defoliant dissemination systems for use in Vietnam. It was General Dwight D. Eisenhower and Grayson Kirk who brought Columbia University's financial support for defense or defense-related projects from less than 1% [in 1945] to about 48% in 1968.

Columbia helped develop the atomic bomb. Its Lamont Geological Observatory under contract maintains a seismograph on the ocean bottom of California for detecting nuclear tests. The military research, secret contracting and defense financing of Lamont and several other Columbia-related research centers are described below.

National Corporations: Administering the Home Country

In a time of turmoil and expansion it is important to maintain a healthy mother country. A well-satisfied domestic population is less likely to question overseas ventures and more willing to take part in their prosecution. Two vital preconditions for a "healthy," smooth-running, industrialized mother country are skilled labor and social stability. The demands of industry are constantly changing and this requires a constantly reeducated population. At the same time some social conflict is inevitable; but the corporate state thinks it has found the means to regulate its direction and intensity.

National corporations' interest and dependency on the university has a long history. The technical-managerial elite that administers private corporations and the government are all products of the universities, particularly their professional schools. To coordinate the complex flow of modern production requires a high degree of professional training. Without engineers and scientists, innovation and adaptation would come to a standstill. Finally, national corporations are most dependent on a consumer-oriented population. Since profit depends on constant expansion it becomes necessary to train more of the population to increasing consumption patterns.

The chart of Columbia's Top 22 reveals primary relationships to leading national corporations (aside from mass media companies) for five of the rulers and several of the others have secondary interests. The Banks which have financial connections with national corporations and hence an interest in their welfare, are also represented on Columbia's Board of Trustees. Because of their business outlook these men have guaranteed the highest priority for the Engineering, Business and Law schools. Consequently, each of these schools has expanded far out of proportion to the other units of Columbia. They spend the most money, maintain the largest plants, and command the most attention from the administration.

Corporation executives have become increasingly aware of the need for social controls over potentially disruptive elements, especially those in the ghetto. Since they are not inclined to invest in low-return operations, they have channeled tax-deductible and foundation funds into the creation of pacification teams trained by the University. The School of Social Work turns out personnel whose approach is ostensibly therapeutic. The standard formula is to convince the disadvantaged that their life difficulties stem from inner sickness rather than disruptive social conditions. This approach treats the poor and potentially rebellious as patients. Instead of removing the cause of their discontent—something that would cost a great deal of money now allocated to overseas priorities—they pacify through treatment. The origins of this therapeutic social work is charity; the effect is to rob the individual of his dignity by requiring him to adjust to intolerable conditions.

Mass media is another form of pacification. By reaching a vast number of people through a limited number of sources, it can create an image of the world that is supportive of the system. To distract is to pacify; the mass media transforms reality into symbols that deaden social awareness. The lock of alternatives creates a climate of coercive persuasion.

Columbia has been instrumental in shaping the mass media industry. New York is the industry's capital and Columbia is its favorite university. Eight of the top 22 are leading figures in major mass communications firms; their influence is mirrored in the size and national status of the Journalism School. The School is well-endowed by the corporations it serves (particularly *The New York Times,* CBS, *Time,* and Cowles publications), and in turn shapes its program to satisfy their needs.

Another function of the mass media is the training of people to develop artificial hunger for mass consumption. As consumption habits become ingrained, the home markets expand. Every blatant or subliminal technique is used to convert natural tastes into the unnatural. This growth in consumption creates high turnover of goods and customers work harder to feed their habits, draining potential monies from those sectors of the population that are already deprived. One of the side effects is to create contempt for property on the part of the already poor minorities. If property is presented as a function of fad, how valuable can it be?

The interdependence between the University and mass media corporations is best exemplified by *The New York Times'* coverage of the April 27th mass arrests on the Columbia campus. Two leading *Times* editorial writers (Gelb and Rosenthal) were secretly briefed by the police and prepared their story long before the actual arrests. The news stories of other *Times* reporters which revealed police brutality were suppressed and the *Times* published editorials favorable to the administration. This was clearly calculated to project a favorable public image for Columbia. Moreover, in the past, A. M. Rosenthal has offered his services to Kirk when the administration needed to rebuff community leaders that were critical of the proposed gym.

Conclusion

The student uprising was the logical and necessary culmination of a long struggle between the propertied and the propertyless, between the powerful and the powerless. Community participation against the university was one of the special features of this struggle. The rebellion mirrored perfectly the growing fight against government policy on a national level.

In order to avoid a clash between property and its function and the community-student opposition, it was necessary to satisfy human needs, but, as the gap between the priorities of the powerful and the powerless widened, as the property needs created inhuman demands and the demands of humanity increased, the only thing that could resolve the issue was, finally, an uprising which seized and redistributed property and, in so doing, redistributed power.

From the pronouncements of the administration, it would seem that these rebellions, at Columbia and other campuses, are unprecedented. Actually, Columbia itself has experienced various kinds of opposition, considered as extreme in their day as the riots appear in our own day. The famous riotous commencement of 1811 resulted in a number of arrests; the Civil War period was wracked by violence over the issue of the draft.

The point of no return for Columbia University in its commitment to the war effort and to profit and property was reached in the coup of 1967 when the academic administrators, Barzun and Chamberlin, were ousted in favor of the managerial manipulators (Truman and Goodell). Now in power are men committed to manipulation, financial and real estate speculation, men on the make.

The generalized fight became hardened and objectified by the surfacing of the IDA and the Morningside Park Gym issues; while they seemed separate, they were ineradically fused, each representing different aspects of property and property drives. The IDA represented commitment to aiding the war effort which, under its anti-communist guise, hunted for new markets in the Communist and third worlds. The gym represented institutional expansion, creation of a service area for empire-building trainees—a frozen negation of domestic, irrelevant populations. Colonialized community and colonialized student needs fused; as an unbearable tension was reached, this new community moved to stop the work on the gym and seized the buildings symbolic of their training and rededicated them to new purposes, seized property and rededicated it to anti-poverty priorities. This action symbolized the need to stop the destructive direction the country was taking.

The students had tried other means before. There had been peaceful demonstrations, pickets, petitions, appeals to debate the issues publicly; there was a questioning of the decision-making rights, appeals to conscience on moral grounds. This earlier stage implied a naïve faith in the democratic process or, rather, that the democratic process worked, went deep and was a part of administration and student body. It was believed that misunderstanding, a basic obtuseness rather than greed and power, motivated the administration; that when the issues were debated freely and openly some kind of rapprochement could be reached. The liberated documents from Grayson Kirk's files revealed that beneath the surface, there had never been democracy and that profit needs, manipuation, were basic to administration behavior.

What were the results of these demands: They were ignored,

they were met with aloofness, professionalism and expertise were interjected (the students were neither trained nor fit to decide these weighty problems of state), arrogance was the order of the day, and when pressures were applied by the student body, suspension was threatened. Implicit in this form of coercion was a death threat: once out of the university, the students were subject to the draft. This process was paralleled in the surrounding community. The University through Morningside Heights, Inc. acted like the lowest slumlord clearing a building to escalate the value, using threats, coercion through law, cutting off heat, involving tenants in long legal struggles, refusing to accept rent and then serving dispossesses. And when protest mounted, symbolic community leaders were chosen from the community who would then negotiate with the administration for concessions that were nothing more than holding actions in an inevitable and total seizure of the community. These leaders had the ground cut out from under them after they had served their purpose . . . and while they dickered for minor victories, their base of power was slowly being eroded. Not content with the Morningside area, the University was moving further and further into Harlem itself, continuing to carve out a huge training enclave to process students to run the empire.

The peculiar feature of Columbia's policy was its hard-line approach, its refusal to deal with legitimate protest at all. In this, other universities have at least been more sophisticated, granting some of the student demands, willing to hold dialogues which, on the surface, seemed meaningful. There has been a smoother interaction, but the struggle has merely been put off, for the other universities will all come to their Columbia uprisings.

Basic to the students' understanding was their understanding of their University position and what the University meant. More and more, defense research defined scholarship. As the needs of international corporate expansion overseas grew for a pool of technicians who shaped material and minds into the proper use-framework, this operation molded curriculum and, in turn, kept the atmosphere proper in a political sense. The schools would be financed if the empire was to be served and if the schools refused to participate, other more pliable schools with officials on the make for money would be found. On the national level domestic markets had to be serviced and people had to be induced more and more to escalate their consumer needs. What this meant on the student level was that, in terms of future expansion needs, the student was a raw commodity that had to be processed into usable forms, had to be made into interchangeable parts on an assembly line basis so that there would be a pool for corporate and defense use. The very creation of this pool insured that there would be intense competition among the trainees and part of this process of preparation for fitting in meant that a preliminary process had to be undertaken, the process of dehumanization, alienation, the creation of a proper subservient mood (subservient in the sense that fierce competition for money and property was permitted, but competition with the system was dangerous and must be considered first neurotic and then subversive. It is no accident that the suicide rates are so high in the universities).

Since priorities were given over to expansion, the community, especially the blacks and Puerto Ricans, were considered irrelevant; investment in this area was too prohibitive since there was easier money to be made elsewhere; i.e., in defense contracts and in the manufacture of high turnover, easily consumable products, war matérial.

As the tensions mounted, legitimacy (legitamcy of the rulers) became illegitimacy when the conflict between maintaining the old legitimacy and satisfying needs indicated that all efforts would have to go into the turning out of goods and the preservation of the property that turned out these goods.

What other way was there, then, to cut through the illegitimate basis of power than to seize the University? And this seizure of property cut through to the raw nerve of the University. Even this might have been mediated but for the liberated documents in Grayson Kirk's office which exposed once and for all, what a sham the appearance of democracy, or paternalistic expertise was. Here was the truth! Here were the secrets! Here was what really went on. The documents undercut all the needs for secrecy justified in the name of national interest. What it was all about was the scramble for money, the fight for markets to make money; what it was all about was manipulation of markets and stock rigging and money plays on the way to power. That the whole defense establishment in all of its manifestations was tied in with corporate interests, tied in with real estate speculation, tied together by contacts, and that the whole process of market escalation was furthered by a series of men on the make who made the decisions that they clothed in the patriotic rhetoric of national security and sanctification of the cold and hot war fight to free the enslaved world. All this was covered by a sanctified university facade which, to the financial detriment of students and faculty, permitted high level robbing to go on without let or hindrance.

The meaning of this seizure of property and the codes of behavior in property protection and accumulation was perceived all too clearly by the administration, especially the crude hard liners who know their operations were the shadiest; realizing they had the most to lose most immediately, the rhetoric gave way to the club. A struggle for survival was mounted by the students and the community as the administration was aided by the overwhelming and ponderous control of almost all the media; history was rewritten as it happened. And, as we have pointed out, it was no coincidence that trustees included Sulzberger of the *Times* and Paley of CBS.

Beatings and jailings followed. The strike represents the lack of recognition of students and community by the powers who rule the University. Student amnesty is a fundamental precondition to settling the strike; it announces and solidifies that the power has shifted in favor of the students and the community, it justifies their cause and creates the grounds for a more formal surrender of power and even the possibility of reshifting the course of the University. It implies the recognition of community needs and if expansion is needed, it argues that expansion must be begun in a way that services the community, the neglected domestic front, and solicits their participation.

The administration's response to student demand was another evasion: establishment due process. The establishment position was clearly defined in this statement by Herbert A. Deane, Vice-Dean of Graduate Faculties (*Spectator*, April 24, 1967). "A university is definitely not a democratic institution. When decisions begin to be made democratically around here, I will not be here any longer." *Spectator* quoted Deane as adding, "Whether students vote 'yes' or 'no' on an issue is like telling me they like strawberries." Appearing to take a softer line, it was the same rulers who appointed the Cox Commission and laid down the ground rules for inquiry—all in an attempt to relegitimize the administrators and the old order. All the members represent the establishment and have establishment hearts. Three are lawyers (Cox, Rifkind, and Amsterdam, a Philadelphia lawer) committed to due process within the rules established by the rulers: no hidden data, such as liberated documents, can enter into the discussion. One, Lewis, is a sociologist whose position, along with the nature of his discipline, presumes objectivity and the viewing of things as they are without moral bias . . . which is to say, keep thing the way they are. The fifth, Dana L. Farnsworth, is the head of Harvard student health services; he has glorified the role of an establishment agent-informer. He has stated, "The psychiatrist and the college police force must often work closely together." For him and for many other psychiatrists, psychiatry in America is a variation of the police function. Whom they cannot adjust they will call mad.

The rebellion has precipitated cleavages among Columbia's rulers. Uris and some of his supporters have insisted on repression. Rockefeller has come out for student dissent. The very crudeness of Uris' action delegitimized the University and the more sophisticated forces have recognized this result. The Rockefellers have longer-range institutionalized interests and can afford the wait that new money cannot: their interests still lie with an overseas empire and they are intently committed to the mass production of technicians and pacifiers. Furthermore, they realize that the domestic front has reached an incredible turmoil. To show the first is to negate the idealistic principles on which this country was founded; suspensions of civil rights would bring people into the fight who, believing that democracy works, wouldn't otherwise join the struggle.

What Columbia meant was that no longer were the weak to be manipulated by the strong, whose revivifying worth was the property they had amassed. They were now open to scrutiny. It became clear that there is a real and legitimate basis for the seizure and redistribution of property to rechannel it into the service of human needs.

Chapter Five

Cambodia, Kent State and Beyond

The beginning of a new decade found the New Left, indeed, the whole radical movement in a state of seeming disarray. Dreams of a revolution and isolated incidents of violence had replaced ideology and organized actions.

With the news of the Cambodian invasion and the deaths at Kent State and Jackson, the political picture was significantly altered. Public response to the invasion, and indeed to the campus shootings, was, at the very least, one of mistrust and uneasiness. There are several possible interpretations of the changed political scene from the New Left point of view. The concluding section will deal with two of them.

Elizabeth and Eugene Genovese perceive that despite its collapse, the New Left succeeded in its goal of political re-education. If indeed a larger portion of Americans are as yet uncommitted to radical forms of action, they may at least be responsive to radical critiques of American society. The Genoveses defend radical criticism, linking it to forms of action in the liberal tradition. They see the beginning of a new opposition.

Langdon Winner and Greil Marcus, however, deny the need for creation of a new opposition; in their article, they describe a revitalized continuity in New Left activism following Cambodia. Rather than perceive the ensuing disorders and disruptions as harmful, they see for the first time the emergence of a unified, reconstituted power for the left.

The National Petition Campaign*

Elizabeth and Eugene Genovese

Each of those who have signed the above petition undoubtedly has his own estimate of its possibilities and significance. We should like to say something about how the statement came to be prepared and give our own view of its possibilities.

Students and faculty members at the University of Rochester reacted to the news from Cambodia and Kent, Ohio, in the same way as their counterparts elsewhere. At a mass meeting on May 5, it was decided to boycott classes and to use the time to discuss what might be done. (The Faculty of the College of Arts and Sciences later voted to support this boycott by students.)

When a campaign in support of this petition was first proposed at this meeting most people reacted with a feeling of *déjà vu*. The proposal seemed trite. But before the discussions were over, most concerned students, including a sizable number of radicals, accepted the petition campaign. They had the support of left-wing faculty members.

The questions raised by skeptical radical students, however, were anything but frivolous, and we should like to review some of the arguments presented by those who decided to support the petition and in fact helped to draft it.

The most striking argument was contained in the observation that we have tried institutional politics and failed. Certainly, the experience of 1968 cannot be recalled with warmth or any sense of great achievement. Since the war has not ended, it could be argued that neither electoral politics nor radical action has worked.

---

* Reprinted with permission from the New York Review of Books.

Yet it is our contention that much has worked. The war in Vietnam is a protracted war for us as well as for those more closely involved in it. The forces of national liberation in Asia and elsewhere know, as Nixon knows, and especially as the unlamented LBJ knows, that the peace movement in the United States has significantly narrowed the Administration's room for maneuver both politically and militarily. Even if we could be certain that all our efforts, perpetually engaged, could not in themselves bring this war to an end, we would retain the duty to press those efforts as a meaningful contribution, whether ultimately small or large, toward the outcome.

But if we grant the need to keep going, what is the point of reopening a struggle on traditional political terrain rather than in the streets? To begin with, it ought to be clear that Nixon's policy has been one of deliberately provoking disorder, especially on the campuses. Agnew's ominous attack on Kingman Brewster coincided with the decision to escalate the war. Nixon's outburst against "bums" on the campus must be read in the same light: the events at Kent State crowned the policy. This policy, if we read it correctly, was designed to make it appear that the opposition to the war is an isolated phenomenon composed of undisciplined middle-class youth—and it is a policy that is now failing.

If the movement can be contained on the campuses, it can be killed on the campuses. If it can be turned into acts of violent frustration of a kind likely to be feared, resented, and certainly misunderstood by the working class and the middle class, then Nixon will surely weather the storm. We believe that there is a Silent Majority in the country—and that it is against the war. But if the resentment and foreboding are to be turned into effective political action, the chasm between the universities, which have been the focus of the antiwar movement, and the community must be bridged. No amount of seized buldings could match the effect of thousands of students and professors going door to door to talk to workers and middle-class Americans. Among other things, face-to-face contact is the best antidote to the fearful and unreasoning reaction of "straight" people to our youth. That reaction has been carefully nurtured by Washington as part of a policy of divide-and-conquer at home.

Undoubtedly, some liberals are ready to leap to support of the petition campaign because they believe it to be a diversionary effort designed to get students off the campuses and to channel their energies into something harmless. It could of course degenerate into that. But consider the response on the University of Rochester campus alone: on a few hours' notice some 800 students, out of a student body of not more than 3,000, collected 8,000 signatures and raised $4,000. At this writing 45,000 signatures have been elicited from the Rochester area alone. One of the accomplishments of the effort was to create the beginnings of a link between campus and community; in the long run, that accomplishment can be consolidated and, if extended across the country, can make a decisive difference.

The frustration that grips our young people, and indeed that touches all of us, has been fed by Nixon's repeated success in rallying the people to each new adventure. Why should this gambit surprise or dishearten us? When the President of the United States goes before the American people and says that he has a plan to end the war and that he needs support, how should we expect them to respond? Let it be remembered, however, that Lyndon Johnson went down that road, and far more effectively than Nixon, until he fell from power. These support-your-President campaigns have their own rhythm, and therein lies Nixon's weakness. Each time the President makes this plea, the majority he rallies is smaller or less dedicated and the time span allowed him is perceptibly shortened.

It is essential, therefore, that the pressure be kept on even as the tactics shift. We must avoid the notion that people are convinced once and for all about the nature of the war and must be prepared to go over every argument, again and again and with the greatest patience.

Most of us, for example, are sick of teach-ins and wonder how much more talk we need. But a teach-in at a local church or community organization that had previously been mindlessly pro-war or indifferent is not the same thing as one more teach-in on a campus where the argument has long been exhausted. A simple device like a petition campaign, properly used, can be the vehicle for reaching two kinds of people: those who have supported the war or are wavering and are willing to listen to new analyses, and those who have been or are now convinced and are ready to take some action. Those who consider signing a petition a meaningless or trival action ought to consider that most Americans have probably never signed a political petition in their lives. For them a decision to do so now and to contribute a few dollars or even a few cents to support peace candidates—it is a decision to take a dramatic first step toward engagement.

But can this kind of political action hold any meaning any more? Even if the petition receives wide support, are we not once more allowing ourselves to be sucked into harmless gestures that government can and will probably ignore?

This is not a call for one more petition, one more Congressional campaign, one more effort to use institutional political machinery. It is a proposal to use a specific political device in order to intercede in a specific political crisis. Many members of Congress are clearly incensed at Nixon's policy. The first result of their reaction has been the cry of "constitutional crisis." Now, clearly, Nixon has not done anything that Truman, Kennedy, Eisenhower, or Johnson did not do before him. But each time the constitutional issue has been fudged, the executive power has been expanded, and the President has been given new powers to pursue predatory policies. That the country is now prepared to review the Presidential power and to concern itself with the question of limiting it can be a major breakthrough and can itself offer new opportunities for popular pressure to restrain, if not defeat, a policy of aggression.

Beyond the constitutional question is the immediate question of staying Nixon's hand. It is naïve to believe that Congressional censure—in one form or another—would not deeply compromise the President. Even if he were to stare it down and continue on course, an open split with Congress would enormously complicate his plans for building a popular center-right coalition. Lyndon Johnson was brought down under far less painful conditions than Nixon can now be made to face. Popular opinion is by no means impotent, but its effectiveness is considerably limited by its division. Many who oppose the war or are sick of it are frightened by the specter of campus disorder or black revolt. Nixon has obscured the antiwar feeling of his own constituency, by a calculated policy of deepening the fear of social disorder. But this strategy could be sorely tried by a general revolt in Congress against his foreign policy.

Unfortunately many congressmen read their constituencies as supporting the President's policy or at least opposing its enemies.

Everything must be done to demonstrate to them that the path of personal political safety is the path of firm opposition. If it is true that the events in Congress, not in general but at this time and under these conditions, are of major importance to the peace movement, then it follows that everything possible must be done to bring popular pressure to bear in support of a general confrontation of Congress with the President.

Many radicals understandably gag on such a strategy. Our best young militants here at Rochester, for example, heatedly and correctly argued that these measures will not in themselves expose the imperialist basis of American policy and may in fact divert the attention of radicals once more into liberal politics. But there is nothing in this or any reasonable alternative strategy that makes such an outcome inevitable. The hard fact is that the New Left has collasped and the Left, Old or New, is in disarray. But the work of the 1960's has not been in vain: a far larger portion of our people is attracted by a radical critique of American society than ever before.

Students and faculty at the University of Rochester are combining in workshops and classes, organized in an "Alternative University," to provide analysis and discussion of community problems. We are determined to use this campaign to build a firm bridge between the university and the community, and so, we understand, are others in universities across the country. The unity and discipline that our students have displayed here have provided hope that a new turn in the fortunes of the Movement can be effected.

Rochester, New York

Elizabeth Fox Genovese
Eugene D. Genovese

How We Spent Our Spring Vacation*

by Langdon Winner & Greil Marcus

BERKELEY—For several weeks previous to the President's announcement of the invasion of Cambodia the University of

* Reprinted with permission by the authors, Rollingstone, June 11, 1970.

California campus was rather vaguely convulsed by a new kind of war games. Tacitly disruptive and occasionally violent anti-ROTC demonstrations took place, seemingly as a spin-off from the more serious activities underway at Stanford. Though the size of the crowds confronting the cops occasionally ranged into the thousands, the mood of those who took part was curious. One saw no rage, anger, horror, fear, or pride; it seemed some of the students were going through familiar paces out of a sense of nostalgia, while others were insistently practicing for future battles. Cops and students kept their distance, the former shooting off their tear gas and the latter throwing rocks.

Cops arrested people at random and forced them to stand in their front lines to take the brunt of other students' rocks. At one point, demonstrators attacked the faculty club and stoned professors, while elsewhere students in class were cut by glass when rocks broke through a classroom window. It was action without context—and it seemed that a pattern of random and unfocused violence was beginning to emerge.

With the announcement of the invasion, events shifted in an extraordinary manner. Berkeley was quiet at first, as if stunned. At Stanford, a student strike that previously had gathered almost no support was able to shut down the school. Strong and unexpected actions on other campuses, especially at Ohio State in Columbus and at the University of Maryland, where students fought with a new ferocity, began to bring events into focus again. By Monday, a small demonstration grew into a larger one as a new assault on the ROTC building took place.

Late in the morning news of massacre at Kent State hit the campus. By Monday night the University was in the process of being shut down without anyone having told it to do so. On Tuesday huge groups of demonstrators roamed all over campus and, after several gas attacks, the administration and police closed the campus.

That night the Academic Senate, long noted for its disregard for student concerns and for its carefully cultivated political impotence, met and voted to condemn the expansion of the war and to urge cancellation of classes for the rest of the week. The university chancellor refused their request with Hayakawa-like pontification about "neutrality", but did, under

pressure, allow a convocation to be held the next day so that
the campus might consider the matter before the nation. At least
15,000 were there on Wednesday.

The extraordinary meeting began with two speeches by
Asian scholars, who pointed out in detail the flaws in Nixon's
rationale for invasion. Speech has not mattered much in radical
politics for several years—rallies have become gathering places
and forums for declamations with little or no intellectual
content. Back in the days of the Free Speech Movement a crisis
always brought a speech that was in fact a sophisticated analysis
of the situation in which we found ourselves, but it had been
a long time since anyone said anything out in public that
told one something he didn't know already. Wednesday was
different. It turned out to be marvelously interesting and truly
exhilarating to be informed by men who knew what they were
talking about. Radical and anti-war professors were finally
filling the role played by Mario Savio years before. We were
not there simply to be harangued, but to find ways to transform
real learning into action.

Still, the anti-war movement at Berkeley had run out of
good ideas. Six years of futile effort had seen the rise and fall
of dozens of tactical moves. Everything from writing one's
Congressman to "trashing" the ROTC building had been tried.
Nothing seemed to work.

The breakthrough came when Professor Sheldon Wolin,
spokesman for the Ad Hoc Faculty-Student Peace Committee,
read the following proposal: "This convocation of students,
faculty and staff of the University of California at Berkeley
declares that this campus is on strike to reconstitute the University as a center for organizing against the war in Southeast
Asia. We are curtailing normal activities for the remainder of
the quarter. We pledge our time, energy and commitment to
stopping this war. We will open the campus to mobilize our
resources—our knowledge and skills, our manpower and facilities. We will organize not only against the war, but against
the structures in society that facilitate that war."

The crowd gave its approval to the Wolin plan with thun-
derous applause. From that point on the idea of "reconstruction"
became a source of liberation and enthusiasm.

The mass meeting broke up and immediately transformed itself into a set of smaller meetings. Students in virtually every department met to plan action for the rest of the quarter. The announcement that Reagan had closed the campus for the week gave us a *fait accompli* that we had to deal with. What the Governor intended as a cooling-off period in fact gave us four days in which to organize. It cut us off from the resources of the University and forced us to salvage and create our own, which we did. Many departments set up headquarters in the fraternity and sorority houses that ring the campus, and went straight ahead into the business of reorganizing our education and setting up for an educational assault into the community at large. We began to realize that the choice of shutting it down was a false one—we would in fact keep it open, but on our terms. We would organize around it if we were locked out —we would subvert it once it was open. Huge numbers of students met all weekend to plan redirection of classes.

It was, of course, the massive convulsion that had shaken the university system across the country that set up the conditions in which we could act with such natural and necessary ease. We realized that it was action in our own communities—not pointless "national" rallies—that mattered. We had to learn how to build politics out of the stuff of our own vocations, our own resources, and our own talents.

The local College of Arts & Crafts had shut itself down days before to immediately re-open as a center making posters and banners for the entire Bay area. Leopolds' Records established a War Surcharge of their own: 25c added to the price of every record, which they matched and made available to the strike fund.

Various departments, now reorganizing under the control of the students and faculty who ignored official authority, reconstituted themselves and began to re-channel their expertise and their time into work that would spread the sense of crisis throughout the community and re-define the permanent concerns of education. Each group attempted to draw on their own talents and expertise. Sociology students utilized their knowledge of social research as they hit the nearby towns of El Cerrito and Albany. Business school students successfully confronted the Bank of America and other large firms, demanding that the corporations poll their employees on the war. In the department of Political Science, literally hundreds of graduates and undergraduates began to investigate sources of potential conflict within the society and to study the effect of the war on the political institutions of society, with the aim of creating a large and accessible body of literature available to students all over the country. The new university looked like a movie by Godard—one he hasn't quite made yet. Through it all ran talk of organizing for a second shut-down next fall, to re-create the conditions of disruption that had opened up so many possibilities.

In the midst of all this activity, most professors stood by and watched and tried to find a role for themselves. We tried to create roles for them, demanding that they abandon their false "neutrality" and teach and speak and organize around their own convictions *as* professors, rather than as de-frocked "individuals." They were on the run.

The spirit of this activity was magnificent. Thousands of students found out that politics involved a re-structuring of virtually all of the assumptions about learning they had brought with them to college. The point was to control and make choices about one's *own* institutions, right here and now. We politicized our own despair about the country—finally arguing with force among ourselves about things that were finally truly at stake, because real things *were* at stake, because we finally had a sense we were gaining power over our own concerns. No more bummer sessions—we were beginning to realize that if one man convinced another real consequences would follow from the fact that a man had changed his mind. Formalism was being replaced by necessity, desire, and imagination.

When school opened again the following Monday it was clear that a significant revolution had taken place. In virtually every department from engineering to zoology, students had banded together and were taking command of their courses.

Chancellor Heyns, a vicious opponent of all student politics, was forced into a hasty capitulation. Yielding to the power of the "reconstitution" movement he ordered the relaxation of the internal rules governing courses, grades and academic procedures. What years of campaigning for university reform had failed to accomplish became a reality overnight. Students could now determine the forms which university life was to take.

The importance of this development cannot be over-emphasized. The primary reason why anti-war activities of the past have always collapsed is that their politics did not become an essential part of the day-to-day existence of the participants. The glorious rallies, election campaigns and marches were merely an exception to the normal pattern. They were artificial roles and masks behind which one could hide and pretend to be committed to the struggle. But when the weekend protest gala was over, everyone removed his radical mask, went back to business as usual and felt guilty.

Under the notion of "reconstitution," this has changed. Students have begun to embrace politics as a central part of their lives. And rather than seek action in unfamiliar contexts and roles, they have begun to take direct control of the conditions which affect their daily lives. They now understand that they do not have to go to the streets to find the agents of political domination. They need confront the authority figures in their lives—their teachers, employers and parents.

No longer need one feel that he must give up his existing identity to become an activist. The point is to "reconstitute" what one has been doing all along—studying, writing, thinking, music, art or whatever else one enjoys most. At Berkeley even those involved in sports began finding ways to make their lives relevant to the new movement. The football team went on strike against spring practice and pledged to transform athletics into a meaningful counter-force to the Cambodian invasion.

Pretty absurd, you say? Just remember that this was the first time in the nation's history in which white athletes had taken a political stand as *athletes*. Think of what might happen if some of Nixon's precious football games were turned into arenas for anti-war protest next fall.

The spirit of reconstitution aims to become peri..anent. In subsequent meetings on the Berkeley campus the idea was defined to include continued militant opposition to American racism, imperialism and all incidents of political repression. Whatever happens in Indochina in coming months, the students have committed themselves to opening as many spheres of American life as possible as space for the new style of politics.

To the media, first there was the Violence Phase, then the Strike Phase, then the March on Washington Phase, and then the Normalcy Go-Work-For-Local-Candidates-Later Phase.

In fact, events were much more confused that that. Violence continued on many campuses all through "Normalcy" Week, and the mass meeting in Washington was an event of the most flatulent triviality and dangerous moderation.

Organized by the same men who created the moratorium movement, this meeting and those that preceded it served only to draw young men and women from their own communities, to lower political consciousness rather than to raise it, to give a false sense of numerical strength, and to encourage the idea that to be political means you "give up" a day of your time every-once in a while. These demonstrations are dangerously moderate because of their fear of offending someone (at the rally in Washington, a group of Kent State students who attempted to lower a flag were stopped by New Mobe marshals and had their "request" referred to "committee"), and because of their fear of recognizing the real conflicts in this society that cannot be smoothed over (at San Jose State a campaign was launched to convince students to cut their hair in preparation to organizing in the community. "We can't show ourselves as we are," said one).

But these mass national demonstrations are most dangerous because they represent politics as "an exception" to normalcy, while students on campuses' all over the nation are in fact attempting to obliterate normalcy as they politicize their own lives. The ease with which the Administration can co-opt and take over for their own purposes both the rhetoric and the activity of moratoriums and "Earth Days" should make it clear that we must develop and maintain forms of political activity that the Administration cannot utilize. We have to move beyond "protest," as students at hundreds of schools are already doing, to a kind of disruption that frees us from normalcy and permits new kinds of action, learning, and knowledge. The following words of a Kent State student have little to do with protest and a great deal to do with the discovery of one's self as a political man ready to *create* a community by defending the *idea* of a community:

"Governor Rhodes said, 'We will meet them with the heaviest force necessary.' And the kids, I think, felt, 'Look, this is our campus.' . . . Well, then they moved into the kids and asked them to leave. But every student probably felt he would be shirking his responsibility to leave . . . giving up and giving in to a kind of military takeover of your campus."

In the foreseeable future the real power of the movement will lie not in its ability to persuade Congress or to win the favor of the voting public. Its effective force will come in its ability to disrupt as many areas of national life as completely and as often as it can.

The reasons for this are not difficult to find. In case after case, the attempts to mobilize Congress and the electorate have failed. At this late date it seems unrealistic to expect that a new moral crusade launched by incensed moderates would have any better chance of success. The majority of Congressmen in fact have a real interest in seeing the war continued. America's military might around the globe is both their ideology and their bread and butter. The nation's public, similarly, has never responded to an appeal based on the immorality of war. After all, how could a conflict which four presidents have endorsed be immoral? The opinion polls show that the public has consistently rallied to each new and ridiculous request by LBJ and Richard Nixon "to support your fighting men in Vietnam." Like sheep in a pasture, the silent majority can be fleeced in this manner about once a month.

Those who examine the matter critically will recognize truth. The only thing that has kept the anti-war movement from perishing altogether in recent years has been its ability to disrupt college campuses and city streets. As it now enters its most crucial stage, the movement must recognize that its primary source of political power lies in its capacity to raise the costs of the war through the conscious disruption of as many areas of American social life as possible.

The specific costs which it can exact are of two basic kinds— economic and psychological. A city, corporation or government bureaucracy must expend tremendous economic resources to repair or prevent the disruption which anti-war militants can cause. As long as the militants pose a threat to the efficient functioning of social processes, funds must be diverted away from other important needs.

The psychological costs are even more devastating. Disrup-

tions brought by anti-war activists have the ability to transform
the American dream into a continuing nightmare. Americans
freak at the sight of demonstrations which reveal to them the
roots of their national guilt. They experience genuine torment
when their illusions of national peace, happiness and good will
are exploded before their eyes. By maintaining the pressure
of radical action, students can show the nation that it cannot
have its wars, international exploitation and racism and still
keep its peace of mind.

The tactics of disruption also has a payoff in its ability to
win new members to the ranks of those who oppose the practices of American domination. They are won over by the sight
of established institutions which can no longer respond to a
meaningful challenge. Any moderately strong jolt to the foundations of our institutions sends them reeling. On university
campuses a great majority of the persons now demonstrating
against the war are former moderates who have learned that
existing structures cannot withstand the moral and political
demands of the times.

The potential effectiveness of the practice of widespread
disruption is also suggested by the most basic fears of our
nation's leaders.

In his speeches and press conferences of the last month or so
Richard Nixon has been obsessed with the idea that America
is becoming "a pitiful helpless giant." The massive American
war machine has failed to achieve its primary goal of "forcing
the Communists to negotiate a lasting peace." The more force
the United States applies, the more desperate the situation looks.

But what exactly is the nature of the American behemoth
that makes it so pitiful and helpless? What is it about the beast
that makes it a prime target for continuous disruption?

Much of it has to do with the giant's own internal make up
—the unbelievable complexity of his nervous system and the
extreme distance between its brain and its long bulky arms.
Each of Nixon's commands must pass through a complex network of communication and bureaucracy before they have any
impact in reality. As they travel through the long and tangled
line of communication, the messages often become perverted
into something different from their original meaning. Nixon

orders "Vietnamization," but the folks out in the field imple-
ment good old-fashioned "Corruption."

As the distance between what is ordered and what is done
increases, the President's plans are reduced to bizarre fantasies. He begins to live in a dream world of rational schemes
which look great on paper but which have no relationship to
reality. Like the fairy tale giant who cannot bend over to pick
up a peanut, he then feels frustrated and strikes out in brutal
rage. Something which cannot be controlled must be crushed.

Nixon's "giant" metaphor also works nicely to describe the
situation at home. American society has indeed become a "pitiful helpless giant"—a vast technological monstrosity which is
now unwieldy to the point of being ungovernable.

Our nation's capitol is now haunted by exactly this idea.
Much of Washington's freakout over the activities following
the Cambodian invasion came from the realization that the
events fit into a long series of horrifying and unpredictable
breakdown in the life processes of this society. Things seem
to be "out of control" and "running amuck" with no apparent remedy in sight. Random chaos became a central part of
American existence.

As the anti-war, anti-racism, anti-imperial movement in
the United States continues to develop, the lessons of Nixon's
"helpless giant" will become more and more evident. The loss
of control in American society is not only a fact of life, it is
also something which can be influenced by one's own actions.
Already saboteurs and system fuckers are at work to aid the
endemic process of breakdown. Through both violent and non-
violent means they have begun to disrupt the flow of communications, electricity, traffic and finance in this country.

The new breed of saboteurs have discovered the crucial
secret of an advanced technological society—that the same
things that make it work are the things that make it vulnerable.

In any modern system the lines of control are very long
and incredibly complex. No single human intellect can com-
prehend the whole system or direct its range of activities. At
any given point in the network there are few if any persons
who actually know what is going on at all. An intelligent person
who has lost faith in the benificence of our large scale systems

can study their technology and uncover points at which they can be disrupted or destroyed in whole or in part. Many have already stumbled upon the key principle—the beast is vulnerable at exactly those points where there exist no back-up mechanism.

In recent months the system fuckers have extended their ingenious work to attacks on computers, power lines and office equipment. The Bay Area has long been the home of a mysterious bomber or bombers who can artfully topple high voltage towers in neat rows of three. Rumor has it that dozens of former Green Berets trained in the techniques of making and using plastic bombs are now organizing themselves for activity in the North-western States. The Pentagon reports an unusually high number of requests for Army training manuals on the theory and practices of sabotage. During last week's anti-war actions, students in Berkeley, Santa Barbara, Maryland, Washington, DC, and New York attempted to stop traffic flow on certain key highways.

Along with the hard core system fuckers the country is seeing the birth of a whole generation of pranksters. The pranksters recognize that our government and private bureaucracies are based on rules of stable expectations, truthfulness and trust. Since there is an immoral war going on, they see no need to abide by such norms. Taking the draft regulations literally, pranksters confuse their draft boards by reporting changes in their status as required by law, e.g., "Gentlemen: Next Friday I plan to visit mother in Portland" or "I think I am developing a corn on my big toe. Will this exempt me from the draft?" Draft boards and the F.B.I. have also been plagued by the frequent report, "I hereby notify you that I have not registered for the draft," mailed in by person who on subsequent check failed to exist. Thousands of the same fictitious persons have bothered airlines by making reservations and then failing to show up. "What after all is a non-person supposed to do?" one of the professional pranksters commented recently.

It will probably be only a matter of time before the system fuckers discover the most effective non-violent tool for disrupting business and government bureaucracies—the telephone. America may come to yearn for the day when all she had to worry about were protests and riots in the streets.